UNDERSTANDING
GISH JEN

UNDERSTANDING CONTEMPORARY AMERICAN LITERATURE
Matthew J. Bruccoli, Founding Editor
Linda Wagner-Martin, Series Editor

Also of Interest

Understanding Alice Walker, Thadious M. Davis
Understanding Bharati Mukherjee, Ruth Maxey
Understanding Chang Rae Lee, Amanda M. Page
Understanding Colson Whitehead, Derek C. Maus
Understanding Edward P. Jones, James W. Coleman
Understanding Jennifer Egan, Alexander Moran
Understanding John Rechy, María DeGuzmán
Understanding Karen Tei Yamashita, Jolie A. Sheffer
Understanding Louise Edrich, Seema Kurup
Understanding Maxine Hong Kingston, Julia H. Lee

UNDERSTANDING

GISH JEN

With a New Preface

Jennifer Ann Ho

THE UNIVERSITY OF
SOUTH CAROLINA PRESS

Cloth and ebook editions published by the University of South Carolina Press, 2015
Paperback edition published in Columbia, South Carolina,
by the University of South Carolina Press, 2023

uscpress.com

Manufactured in the United States of America

32 31 30 29 28 27 26 25 24 23
10 9 8 7 6 5 4 3 2 1

Library of Congress Cataloging-in-Publication Data
can be found at http://catalog.loc.gov/

ISBN 978-1-61117-588-2 (cloth)
ISBN 978-1-61117-589-9 (ebook)
ISBN 978-1-64336-423-0 (paperback)

This book is dedicated to the many students I have had the privilege of teaching. I may have been the instructor of record in the classroom, but I learned so much from all of you.

I've always been interested, in my books, not only just in capturing the Chinese-American experience, but the whole American experience.

Gish Jen, "The Chinese Experience: Personal Journeys Interview with Bill Moyers," *Becoming American*

CONTENTS

SERIES EDITOR'S PREFACE

The Understanding Contemporary American Literature series was founded by the estimable Matthew J. Bruccoli (1931–2008), who envisioned these volumes as guides or companions for students as well as good nonacademic readers, a legacy that will continue as new volumes are developed to fill in gaps among the nearly one hundred series volumes published to date and to embrace a host of new writers only now making their marks on our literature.

As Professor Bruccoli explained in his preface to the volumes he edited, because much influential contemporary literature makes special demands, "the word understanding in the titles was chosen deliberately. Many willing readers lack an adequate understanding of how contemporary literature works; that is, of what the author is attempting to express and the means by which it is conveyed." Aimed at fostering this understanding of good literature and good writers, the criticism and analysis in the series provide instruction in how to read certain contemporary writers—explicating their material, language, structures, themes, and perspectives—and facilitate a more profitable experience of the works under discussion.

In the twenty-first century Professor Bruccoli's prescience gives us an avenue to publish expert critiques of significant contemporary American writing. The series continues to map the literary landscape and to provide both instruction and enjoyment. Future volumes will seek to introduce new voices alongside canonized favorites, to chronicle the changing literature of our times, and to remain, as Professor Bruccoli conceived, contemporary in the best sense of the word.

Linda Wagner-Martin, Series Editor

PREFACE

I'm delighted to write the preface to the paperback edition of *Understanding Gish Jen* because it is truly a delight to dive into Jen's works. Jen is a master wordsmith, a brilliant storyteller, and a trenchant observer of contemporary US society. Since *Understanding Gish Jen* was released in 2015, Jen has published three more books and several short stories, opinion pieces, and essays. Though this brief preface cannot do justice to the works Jen has produced from 2015 to 2022, I will attempt to distill the major themes of the three books and contextualize them against one another and within her overall literary oeuvre.

The Girl at the Baggage Claim: Explaining the East-West Culture Gap (Vintage 2017) is, in many ways, an extension and expansion of the 2012 Massey lectures that Jen delivered at Harvard University, which were published as a single volume in *Tiger Writing: Art, Culture, and the Interdependent Self* (Harvard University Press 2012). Like *Tiger Writing*, *Girl at the Baggage Claim* is a nonfiction work and thus a departure for what Jen, as a purveyor of fictional narratives, is most known for. To return to the adjective that best encapsulates Jen's writing, it is delightful to see what piques Jen's intellectual curiosity and follow the peregrinations of her mind as she considers the interdependent versus the independent self and the ambidependence that is the middle way between the binaries. While Jen uses the language of "East" to discuss the interdependent self and "West" to talk about independence, she is also careful not to reify stereotypes of all Asians being interdependent and all white Euro-Americans being independent.

Though this may not have been Jen's intent when she wrote it, what *Girl at the Baggage Claim* does most expertly is give readers a glimpse into the mind of a creative writer: the contemporary issues that Jen is most invested in and that are evident in her fictional narratives. Much of her fiction depicts the tensions that occur with Asian American characters who are navigating between Asian-ethnic traditions and US American norms. Though scholars, like myself, are wary of such binaries, it would also be inaccurate not to recognize that there can be grains of truth in stereotypical statements like Asians are more community oriented or US Americans are driven by rugged individualism. Jen shares the research and reading she has done on this subject, including a long list of secondary sources she consulted. As a work that is attempting to serve as a bridge between social psychology and the public, I appreciated the push of *Baggage Claim* in challenging my thoughts about the various social and cultural factors that contribute to the identities of hyphenated people, such as Asian Americans who live between and among the pressures of community and family obligations alongside personal desires for an authentic self.

Turning to Jen's fifth novel *The Resisters* (Knopf 2020), like *The Girl at the Baggage Claim* this is new territory for Jen, which I was delighted to see because it's thrilling when an author takes risks and goes outside of their typical terrain—in this case, writing a work of speculative fiction that may be not so much speculative as prescient given the direction of the United States as of the writing of this preface. *The Resisters* is set in a dystopian future in which bees and birds are extinct, the United States is now the United States of AutoAmerica, and society is divided into "netted" (people with privilege who are producers) and "surplus" (minorities of many stripes who are relegated to being consumers). Told from the first-person perspective of Grant Cannon-Chastanet, a surplus former professor who describes himself as "coppertoned," of Black Caribbean background, Grant is married to Eleanor, a Chinese Irish lawyer, described as "spy-eyed," and father to Gwen, a "Blasian" girl (in the language of the novel) and baseball wunderkind whose pitching prowess serves as the central plot device for the novel.

The Resisters is the most pointedly political of Jen's novels in that it is the most overtly engaged with social justice themes, such as a critique of capitalism and its ties to white supremacy in the form of the "angelfair"—netted people who go through a "PermaDerm" process reminiscent of George Schulyer's *Black No More* (1931) such that the people of privilege are literally white skinned. The surplus, those who escape the "ShipEmBack" policy of AutoAmerica, are a motley multiethnic and multiracial underclass, who live in floating townships and are monitored by the AutoNet that rules AutoAmerica referred to as "Aunt Nettie" by the Cannon-Chastanets. The dystopia of *The Resisters* has its roots in twenty-first-century US policies and Supreme Court decisions, such as allowing corporations to be considered a class of people protected by the Fourteenth Amendment and the deterioration of privacy in favor of technological convenience. The novel's title is inspired from the persona of Eleanor, who files multiple lawsuits with her volunteer team of attorneys against AutoAmerica over the environmental damages that Surplus people face in the food they eat and the toxicity of the land. Although there is a lot of darkness in the novel, Jen's trademark wit and warmth leavens the heavier parts of the novel, especially in the baseball scenes where Gwen gets to shine and excel. And in the spirit of all good sports narratives, *The Resisters* illuminates how baseball is not just a leisure sport but a means for fighting and resilience. Baseball allows Gwen, a feminist multiracial icon, to rise up and for netted and surplus alike to resist the powers of inhumanity and authoritarianism.

One would not be surprised for Jen to take a well-deserved break after publishing two books within three years, yet two years after *The Resisters* came Jen's ninth book and second short story collection *Thank You Mr. Nixon* (Knopf 2022), which coincided with the fiftieth anniversary of Richard and Pat Nixon's historic visit to China. With eleven linked short stories, Jen's latest book contains original works and previously published fiction from earlier in her career, "Lulu in Exile" (*New York Times Magazine* 1998), "Duncan in China" (*Who's Irish?* 1999), "Amaryllis" (*Paris Review* 2006), and "Gratitude" (*Ploughshares* 2006) and work that was published more recently, "No More Maybe" (*New Yorker* 2018), "Mr. Crime and Punishment and War and Peace" (*Yale Review* 2019), and "Detective Dog" (*New Yorker* 2021). The title story is the first and the pivot for which all subsequent stories revolve: the opening of relations between the United States and China in which Tricia Sang, whose American name is taken from Pat Nixon, writes a letter from heaven to the former US president thanking him for coming to China and inspiring her to produce coats for mass consumption—ones that she designed based on the red coat worn by Pat Nixon when she joined her husband on that fateful trip.

Arranged in chronological order from the 1970s to 2020, Jen's short stories are told from a variety of perspectives and locations, with the four-year-old daughter of an interracial Chinese-Cuban couple traveling to China in "It's the Great Wall!" showing up as a forty-year-old unmarried New Yorker engaged in an online affair in "Amaryllis." Some of the characters are living paycheck to paycheck, while others are wealthy enough to buy the adjoining apartments in a luxury high rise during the COVID-19 pandemic. Most interesting to note, details from Jen's research in *The Girl at the Baggage Claim* are woven into her fiction, such as the Chinese reproducing/forging great works of art, which she talks about in chapter 6, "Boundary Blurring," about the Dafen Oil Painting Village, a place where Chinese artists mass produce masterworks of Renoir, Monet, and Klimt (among others). In "Rothko, Rothko" one such artist, living in the United States and painstakingly recreating the painting technique and art of Mark Rothko, is trying to survive, and Jen's story makes readers consider whether the Chinese woman is an artist, a forger, or perhaps a bit of both. And as many reviewers have noted, the work that closes the collection, "Detective Dog," is a tour-de-force, capturing the claustrophobia, fear, and anxiety of the global pandemic and revealing that even those who seemingly have limitless resources are still humans trying to connect with other humans, in all our foibles and frailty.

There's a distinct possibility that by the time this preface is published, Jen will have written more short works and perhaps even published another book, such is the prolific nature of this marvelous contemporary US author. I cannot wait to consume more of Jen's writing, whether it's a return to her social science interests in how humans are shaped by their environments or in the stories she weaves, in short and long form. Writing is the core of who Jen is, as she shared about her craft in a recent interview with *The Articulate Show* (season 6; episode 3; December 4, 2020): "It's my home. I'm a fish in water, and that's what I was put on earth to do."

ACKNOWLEDGMENTS

The first person I have to thank is Gish Jen. As a literary critic I appreciate her books as wonderful texts to analyze. As a teacher I rely on her novels to provide valuable lessons for my students. As one who loves to read, I have been delighted by her works over the last two decades. It has been such a pleasure to reread her novels and discover new short fiction and essays, and I anticipate future reading enjoyment for years to come. I also have to thank Linda Wagner-Martin for giving me the opportunity to write this book. Linda has been an amazing mentor, colleague, and friend; I am very appreciative of the many ways she has supported me in my career. The bulk of the writing for *Understanding Gish Jen* was accomplished in the summer of 2014, when my weekly writing group helped to keep me on target; so thank you, Gabrielle Calvocaressi, Heidi Kim, Angeline Shaka, Karla Slocum, Jenny Tone-Pah-Hote, and Margaret Weiner. I also have to thank my other writing buddy, Ariana Vigil, whose encouragement and friendship have sustained me during our Friday writing sessions at the Looking Glass Café and in my day-to-day life. And to Rebecca Walsh, a big note of gratitude for the key work breaks of films, zucchini fries, and World Cup soccer that sustained me during my relentless summer writing schedule. Finally, the person to whom I owe the greatest debt of gratitude is my husband, Matthew Grady. As I made the last push on this manuscript, he kept me fed and he kept me sane. These words cannot capture how much I appreciate all that he means to me, but hopefully they are a small way of saying I love you.

CHAPTER 1

Understanding Gish Jen

Gish Jen is an American writer. She also happens to be an Asian American writer, and specifically she is an American writer of Chinese descent. While it might be tempting to pigeonhole her work as Chinese American, Asian American, or ethnic American literature, Jen's writing exceeds the bounds of those categories even as it provides exemplary literary representations of Chinese American, Asian American, and ethnic American life. As Jen said in an interview with fellow contemporary American and Asian American writer Don Lee, "I have hoped to define myself as an American writer."[1]

Lillian Jen was born on Long Island, New York, on 12 August 1955, the second of five children, three boys and two girls. Her parents were Chinese immigrants from Shanghai, and in the United States her father, Norman, worked as a civil engineer while her mother, Agnes, taught elementary school. The Jen family moved from Long Island to Queens and then to Yonkers, where Jen attended a Catholic school with a library that contained only a single shelf of books. Despite the paucity of reading material at her school, Jen developed a love of both reading and writing. In the fifth grade Jen had her first story published in the class's literary magazine; it was a tale "about a maid who had stolen some gold. She had hidden it inside this hat, but when she picked up the hat, the gold fell out!"[2] Even in this first literary offering, Jen's trademark wit and comic sensibility are in evidence. Among Jen's earliest literary influences, Louisa May Alcott's *Little Women* and Jane Austen's *Pride and Prejudice,* one can see how these novels of female domestic life left their mark on Jen, as her own work would tackle similar small family dramas that reveal larger social, political, gender, and in Jen's case racial and ethnic dynamics.

It was also while she was in the fifth grade that Jen's family moved once again, this time to the more affluent community of Scarsdale, New York, which

Jen would come to fictionalize as Scarshill in her second novel, *Mona in the Promised Land* (1996). Like Yonkers, Scarsdale did not have a sizable Chinese or Asian American presence, but it did have a Jewish community, which would come to influence her fictional world making in *Mona*. No longer having to make do with a single library shelf, Jen indulged her reading passions by checking out two books a day from her new school library and expanding her literary tastes with texts such as Albert Camus's *The Stranger*. While in high school Jen continued her writerly ambitions by becoming the literary editor of the school magazine. Most notably, it was while she was in high school that Lillian Jen became Gish Jen, a nickname bestowed on her by friends inspired by the silent movie actress Lillian Gish. Describing the rationale for changing her name, Jen explained, "My friends thought Gish Jen was a better name because it had more of an impact. It sounds strong because of the spondee 'Gish Jen': like 'bang, bang.' I always associate 'Lillian' with a shyer self, a received self."[3] Here we can see another literary theme that Jen would take up in her writing: the ability to rename and remake yourself into an identity that you choose versus one bestowed on you from birth.

After graduating from high school, Jen made her way north to Cambridge, Massachusetts, where she attended Harvard University. Citing pressure from her parents, Jen began her scholarly life with a focus on medicine, but during the semester that she was enrolled in English 283, a legendary prosody course taught by Robert Fitzgerald, she switched majors when Fitzgerald helpfully observed, "Why are you premed? . . . I suggest you consider doing something with words."[4] After switching her premed major (in which she was getting a C in chemistry) to prelaw, Jen eventually graduated with a B.A. in English literature in 1977 and with Fitzgerald's assistance acquired a job at Doubleday Publishing in New York City.

Although working at Doubleday enabled her to do "something with words," her year at the publishing house did not leave her feeling fulfilled professionally or financially: "I realized I had found myself in some middle ground. I was neither doing what I really wanted to do, nor was I making any money."[5] Realizing that she was more interested in spending her days talking about the latest *New Yorker* short story and other matters of fiction with her coworkers, Jen decided to take a practical approach to changing careers by applying to universities that had M.B.A. programs and that were also strong in creative writing. In 1979 she matriculated into Stanford University, where she would meet her future husband, David O'Connor, during orientation. While her classmates spent their days on business case studies, Jen immersed herself in taking writing classes and reading novels: "I think it's safe to say that I was the only first-year business school student who read a hundred novels while she was at business school."[6] Although she passed her first year (which Jen credits as coming solely through the coaching of her husband the night before exams), Jen dropped out of the M.B.A. program at the beginning of her second year after she continually overslept and missed attending her classes.

While Jen never regretted leaving Stanford, her decision was not without consequences. Four of the five Jen children attended Ivy League schools; Jen's three brothers would become successful businessmen, and her sister became the doctor of her parents' dreams. Disappointed in Jen's career choice, her parents cut her off financially and emotionally: they no longer paid her bills, and her mother stopped talking to her for a year and a half. In need of an income and with a desire to visit her parents' homeland, Jen found a position teaching English at the Shandong Mining College in Jinan, China. Her time in China enabled her to learn Mandarin, although by her own admission, "I don't speak very well and I don't understand that well anymore these days. I've never been very good at it"; and it inspired her short story "Duncan in China," an original composition published in her short story collection *Who's Irish?* (1999).[7] China is also where Jen's understanding about her ethnicity and her parents' heritage became pronounced: "I really began to understand that certain strains of thoughts in my parents and in myself were Chinese. In some ways, I didn't even know what my conflicts were until I went to China—what it means to be Chinese; what it means to be American; what it means to be Chinese American."[8]

In 1981 Jen entered the famed Iowa Writers' Workshop at the University of Iowa. When asked about her time there, she cited the positive influence of the instructors Bharati Mukherjee and James Alan McPherson: "Writing school often focuses on technique, which is important, but I feel lucky that I met a couple of people who also cared about content."[9] While she said that she did not feel ostracized due to her racial or ethnic difference, she noted that "in my year there were a lot of cowboys. So I did feel like an outsider, but interestingly it wasn't SO much because I was an Asian-American.[10] I felt like an outsider because I was from the east, and I had gone to Harvard and that was not cool the year I was there."[11] After earning her M.F.A. in 1983, Jen married David O'Connor and moved to California, where O'Connor was working at Apple Computers. When his next job took him to Cambridge, Massachusetts, Jen found herself in 1985 applying for secretarial positions at her alma mater since she was not sure if her literary career would ever take off. Lucky for Jen, she was also applying for fellowships at the same time, and the day she received a phone call from Harvard offering her a position as a typist, she also received a letter informing her that she would be a 1986 Radcliffe Bunting Fellow. This fellowship would confirm her literary prowess and become the first of her many notable literary accomplishments.

In 1986 Jen's short story "In the American Society" was published by the *Southern Review*. This was a significant milestone since it was in this story that readers were introduced to the Chang family and that the seeds for her first novel, *Typical American*, were sown. In 1987 the Chang family made another appearance in "The Water Faucet Vision," published in the literary journal *Nimrod*. It would go on to be selected by the guest editor Mark Helprin for Houghton-Mifflin's *Best American Short Stories 1988*, the first of three stories by Jen that would be bestowed this honor. With her credentials firmly established in the short fiction realm, Jen would see the publication of her first novel, *Typical American*, in 1991 with Houghton-Mifflin. This novel takes place in the mid- to late twentieth century and concentrates on three Chinese immigrants who find themselves becoming American: Ralph, Theresa, and Helen. In the world of Jen's fiction, *Typical American* is the novel that has the most "historic" setting, in terms of not taking place in the contemporary moment of when Jen was writing. However, despite its setting in the recent past, its attention to Chinese American / Asian American characters is a theme that Jen would return to in future stories and novels. As Jen has explained, "I did feel it was important that there be Asian American representation in literature. I didn't see that it limited my subject matter in any way. There's nothing I couldn't write about using Asian American characters."[12] *Typical American* launched Jen's literary career: it was short-listed for the National Book Critics Circle Award and was named a *New York Times* Notable Book.

While *Typical American* earned many distinctions, it was also a book that reviewers often lumped together with other Asian American books published that same year. One *Publishers Weekly* article, "Spring's Five Fictional Encounters of the Chinese American Kind," discussed Jen's novel alongside four other Chinese American narratives (Frank Chin's *Donald Duk*, Gus Lee's *China Boy*, David Wong Louie's *The Pangs of Love*, and Amy Tan's *The Kitchen God's Wife*) that also came out in 1991. Jonathan Yardley, writing for the *Washington Post Book World*, similarly observed that the other Chinese American novels published in the same year as *Typical American* are "good books all dealing, in their different ways, with much the same subject."[13] To an outsider, one unfamiliar with the variety and vastness of Asian ethnicities in the United States or the regional and temporal differences of Chinese immigrants arriving in the United States from the late nineteenth century through the late twentieth century, Jen's novel may well seem to deal with the same subject matter as Frank Chin's magical realist novel about a fifth-generation Chinese American boy traveling back in time to the building of the transcontinental railroad or Gus Lee's coming-of-age story of a young boy growing up in the postwar United

States in the African American neighborhood of the San Francisco panhandle. But as Jen has trenchantly observed, "When people look at a picture by Cezanne, no one's really interested in the apples. They're interested in the way in which he has transformed those apples. But if you're an Asian American writer, people are not interested in the quality of artistic transformation; they're interested in your *material*. There's a sense in which we're all writing immigrant autobiographies. The work is not valued as art; it's valued as what is called 'social documentary.' I find that very frustrating."[14]

It is significant that Jen calls herself an Asian American writer rather than a Chinese American writer; this invocation signals her recognition of race and the ways that writers of Asian ancestry, regardless of their ethnic specificity or length of time living in the United States, are subject to certain assumptions, for example that they all come from immigrant families. Besides countering these kinds of stereotypes, Jen, like other Asian American and nonwhite contemporary American writers, is often asked if she is (or is assumed to be) writing veiled autobiography: "people will always say, 'Oh it must be your family,' but in fact it's not my family I wrote about."[15] Yet she has continually emphasized that the Changs are an entirely fictional creation and has often related, in interviews, how her mother read her first novel and was glad to see that there was no one she recognized in any of the characters in *Typical American*: "My mom got to the end of *Typical American* in galleys, and she said, 'Ahhh! So well written!' And then she said, 'And it's not about anybody!'"[16] Her mother's comment, which Jen says is among her favorite reviews, signals that Jen's inspiration was drawn from her imagination; it is her craft as an artist and not her ethnic identity that *Typical American* affirms.

Jen has also elaborated on her frustration with the ways in which she and other Asian American writers are pigeonholed into writing about ethnographic concerns or expected to provide a glimpse into the world of an Orientalist Asia. She recounted a letter she received from the *Paris Review* rejecting her writing about Asian Americans with the explanation, "We prefer your more exotic work."[17] But Jen did not capitulate to these critiques: "I was writing against the public's expectation as I understood it. I was damned if I was going to give them the exotic nonsense they thought they wanted; instead, I wanted my book to succeed on character. I followed my own interests."[18] Her writing interests, as amply demonstrated from her considerable fictional output, have been concerned with all things American (identities, histories, families, experiences, immigration, politics, race, gender, class), but she has also reacted to the ways in which she is seen as somehow less than a true or typical American: "There's not a sense that Saul Bellow's characters are less American than John Updike's.

But there is a perception that my characters are less American than Updike's. And that's the kind of thing I'm questioning. How is it that Bellow is writing about America, and I'm writing about the Asian American experience?"[19]

Indeed first and foremost Jen is an American writer par excellence, one who shares the distinction of being included among the best of short fiction writers. Her story "Birthmates," originally published in *Ploughshares,* was selected by the guest editor Jane Smiley for *The Best American Short Stories 1995.* It was further honored by having John Updike include it in *The Best American Short Stories of the Century* alongside the likes of such literary luminaries as Ernest Hemingway, William Faulkner, F. Scott Fitzgerald, Richard Wright, Philip Roth, Cynthia Ozick, Raymond Carver, and Alice Munro. In many ways her second novel, *Mona in the Promised Land* (1996), announces its American roots most clearly through its subject matter and through Jen's intention to, in fellow writer Don Lee's words, "complicate" what it means for her to be an Asian American writer by focusing on the second generation of the Chang family, particularly the youngest daughter, Mona, and her newly formed identity as a Chinese Jewish American girl growing up in suburban New York of the 1970s.[20] Like her first novel, *Mona in the Promised Land* grew out of a short story, "What Means Switch?" (originally published in 1990 in the *Atlantic Monthly*), and while it continues to engage with the Chang family, it departs from *Typical American* by keeping the central focus on Mona's teenage adventures and identity explorations. Although *Mona* was met with mixed reactions from some reviewers, who seemed confused that Jen would be writing about a Chinese American girl's conversion to Judaism against a backdrop of civil rights activism and comic undertones, it was named a *New York Times* Notable Book and solidified Jen's credentials as a uniquely American writer.

Jen's short fiction has been published in the *New Yorker,* the *Atlantic Monthly,* the *Yale Review, Fiction, Ploughshares,* and the *Iowa Review,* to name just a sampling of literary venues. Therefore it was no surprise that she would follow her two novels by publishing a collection of short stories, *Who's Irish? Stories* (1999), which features two new stories ("Duncan in China" and "House, House, Home") as well as previously published works of short fiction (among them the two stories selected in the *Best American Short Story* collections, "Birthmates" and "The Water Faucet Vision"). Jen credits *Typical American* and *Mona in the Promised Land* and the reception both novels have received in allowing her to branch out in her prose by taking on the perspective and voice of a Chinese immigrant woman in the title story, "Who's Irish?" Alluding to the common misperception that Asians in America are not native speakers, Jen has noted that after publishing for over a decade with characters speaking Standard English, she could finally render Chinese immigrant speech in her fiction: "I could not have written this story early on in my career in dialect, using that voice, because if I had sent it out, the assumption would have been that I didn't speak English. I'm sure some editor would have sent it back to me, saying, 'Oh, well, you know, when your English is a bit better.'"[21] Noting that the charge of not being "American" enough or the assumption that English is not one's first language is a perennial problem for Asian American writers, Jen has observed that this tension illustrates "where the inner self bumps up against society. We're all constructs, we're all compromises between what we've experienced and how we're perceived."[22]

In Jen's fourth book, *The Love Wife* (2004), she returns to the novel form, but she continues to branch out as a writer by having her narrative contain multiple homodiegetic, first-person character-narrators. Rather than the singular omniscient narrator (which marked her first two novels) or the solo first-person narrators of some of her short fiction, Jen employs a new technique by having each chapter narrated by a member of the Wong family: Chinese American husband and father Carnegie Wong; his white wife, referred to as "Blondie" in the novel; their Asian adopted daughters Lizzy (fifteen years old, left at a church doorstep) and Wendy (nine years old and adopted from China); and Lan, a Chinese immigrant and the titular "Love Wife" whom Carnegie's mother sends to live with the Wong family. Each of these characters (minus the mixed-race baby Bailey, who is thirteen months when the novel opens) narrates at multiple points in each chapter, creating a polyphonic tale formed out of various focalizations that overlap and intertwine. *The Love Wife* demonstrates Jen's virtuosity as a creative writer to continue exploring her craft by playing with voice and perspective.

World and Town (2010), Jen's fifth book, returns to omniscient narration and features her most mature and reflective protagonist, Hattie Kong, a biracial white-Chinese (or Eurasian, as she is described in the novel) woman in her late sixties whose white mother was an American missionary in China. Hattie finds herself widowed and retired in a small New England town and assisting an immigrant Cambodian family, newly arrived to Riverlake, as a way to cope with her loneliness. Yet while reviewers have noted the themes of aging and identity and the permutations of grief that undergird *World and Town,* her trademark wit and comic sensibility are still in evidence through her portraits of small-town politics (there is lively debate and dissension about the building of a cell phone tower in their town) and the reciprocal misunderstandings that occur between typical Americans (be they white or Asian American) and newly arrived immigrants. Reviews of *World and Town* are overwhelmingly laudatory of Jen's masterful prose voice and are confirmed through her being awarded the Massachusetts Book Award for her fourth novel.

While Jen's literary output, in terms of her novels and short fiction, speaks to her literary prowess, the awards and accolades she has amassed over the past three decades affirm her place as a contemporary American writer of renown. In addition to the awards listed above, she has received a Guggenheim Fellowship, a Fulbright award to China, the prestigious and lucrative Mildred and Harold Strauss Living Award through the American Academy of Arts and Letters (a prize that carries a fifty-thousand-dollar honorarium every year for five years), and an honorary Ph.D. from Emerson College. In addition she has been named a fellow at the American Academy of Arts & Sciences. Most recently Jen was asked to present at her alma mater a series of talks, the Massey Lectures, which focus on the history of American civilization. These three talks were collected and edited into her sixth book, *Tiger Writing: Art, Culture, and the Interdependent Self* (2012). Jen's latest work solidifies her place as both a contemporary American fiction writer and a public intellectual, a place that is also evidenced by the number of Jen's essays and articles regularly featured in mainstream media outlets such as the *New York Times,* the *Atlantic Monthly,* and the *New Republic.* Her reputation as a master at the short story form was further cemented when yet another of her stories, "The Third Dumpster" (originally published in 2012 in *Granta*), was selected by the guest editor Elizabeth Strout for *The Best American Short Stories 2013.*

Jen is an artist of remarkable skill who writes with an engaging, sardonic, and imaginative prose voice, creating memorable and lively characters and illuminating themes common to the American experience: immigration, assimilation, individualism, the freedom to choose one's path in life, and the complicated relationships we have with our families and our communities. She was featured as one of seven novelists in PBS's *American Masters* series "The American Novel: Novel Reflections on the American Dream," in which her novel *Typical American* was explicated by notable critics and writers, who described her protagonist Ralph Chang as an everyman immigrant (Andrew Delbanco), compared him to iconic American characters such as Jay Gatsby and Nick Carraway (Julia Alvarez), and charted his pursuit of the American dream (Richard Yarborough).[23] Jen was also featured as a subject in Bill Moyers's series "Becoming American: The Chinese American Experience," in which the two discussed Jen's life from her parents' courtship and immigration from China to the United States, to her struggles with finding her path as a fiction writer, to her current life as a contemporary author living in Cambridge, Massachusetts, with her Irish American husband and their two mixed-race children, Luke and Paloma. Moyers and Jen spent a considerable amount of time on the latter topic, which became a theme within Jen's later fiction, *The Love Wife* and *World and Town.*

Jen is unique among the pantheon of contemporary American writers in the number of times her works have been anthologized and referred to in pedagogy articles, which makes her a regular presence in college classrooms across the United States. However, her place in the university classroom is not simply through her texts but is also in her own presence as a visiting instructor of creative writing, as she has taught both nationally and internationally in such select schools as Brandeis University, the University of Hong Kong, Beijing Normal University, Harvard University, Central European University in Prague, the University of Massachusetts in Boston, and Tufts University. Jen is both a writer's writer and a scholar's writer; the technical mastery of her prose along with the themes she engages in—immigration, acculturation, gender norms, sexual norms, family tension, the American dream—make her popular among both general readers and literary critics, who mine her works for the intellectual richness that her fiction demonstrates. The catalog of anthologies, edited collections, literary readers, and journal articles in which her short fiction and novels have been excerpted or analyzed speaks to the importance of her literary voice as representing the best of contemporary American writing and to how accessible, philosophical, and thought provoking her fiction is. Her observations about life in the United States through the perspectives of her Asian American and Asian immigrant characters resonate with various audiences who want to learn something about life as an Asian in America as well as see themselves reflected in the universal themes of love, grief, desire, disappointment, and general domestic experiences that guide all our lives.

Jen is dedicated to her craft as an American creative writer. She also recognizes her responsibility as a minority author in a mainstream world where "American" is often taken to be synonymous for "white." Speaking about the atmosphere of racial and ethnic diversity that has developed over the decades since she first began writing, Jen observed, "One of the good things that's emerged from multiculturalism is that people don't feel they can write whatever they want and then hide behind artistic license. You're forced to consider what you do unconsciously, and I think that's good for writers. I'm not against artistic freedom, but there's a moment for every writer when you bring things out in public and look at them. I think now we look with new eyes, and that makes for better fiction."[24]

Certainly Jen's is among the better fiction in our contemporary times, as she is among the earliest of contemporary Asian American writers to be published, let alone acknowledged for the strength of her prose voice. While she has been critical of reviewers stereotyping her works and not recognizing her fiction as being part of the American literary fabric, she is also well aware of how people of color are portrayed in literature and believes that her work should be mindful of that history: "I support social responsibility in writing. I think I'm a rare writer in saying that. Most writers argue for artistic freedom. But to imagine that your images have no effect on what happens in society and the way people see themselves is completely naive. I think also that you are a better writer as you start considering questions like *representation*. I don't see how writing stereotypes about blacks or Asians or anybody else could possibly make you a better writer. The whole way of writing that used to be popular—in which there is a black and a white, a good guy and a bad guy, and certain people or races get to be the bad guys—is very unfortunate and stupid. We live in a much more complicated world."[25] Jen's artistry as a contemporary writer lies in the liveliness of her prose and her prowess as a fiction writer. She may populate her fiction with characters of Asian descent, but they are quintessentially American—uniquely Asian American.

CHAPTER 2

Typical American
Immigrant American Dreams

Gish Jen's debut novel begins with the declaration, "It's an American story."[1] This opening line, coupled with the title of this work, *Typical American,* alerts readers to the central theme of her first book. What they will encounter in the pages that follow is a story that engages with the spirit of America: of dreams chased, of challenges surmounted, of individual spirit, and the darker sides of these pursuits. As Jen has noted, "When I wrote that opening line, 'This is an American story,' I was redefining an American tradition. That's one level of my book. As an Asian American, I understood that I was going to be ghettoized, and I wanted to get out."[2] As one of the pioneering voices in contemporary Asian American literature, Jen in her first novel declares to readers that regardless of whether she is ghettoized or not, she considers herself and her characters to be quintessentially American: "I wanted to challenge ideas of what a 'typical American' looks like, to put forward the idea that the Changs are not any less American than anyone else. There are people who, when they choose to read ethnic writing, want comfortably exotic stuff that makes them feel like they're traveling in some foreign country. The Changs, though, are not a foreign country. They wonder about their identity: they ask themselves who they are, who they're becoming. And therefore they are American."[3]

The characters of *Typical American* made their first appearance in two of Jen's short stories, "In the American Society" (1986) and "The Water Faucet Vision" (1988). Both stories are focalized through the eldest daughter's, Callie, homodiegetic narration and describe events in the life of the Chinese American Chang family. Yet in *Typical American* (1991), Jen employs a heterodiegetic, omniscient narrator instead of the first-person voice of Callie, which allows her to focus on the actions and inner lives of the three adult members of the Chang family: the patriarch Ralph; his sister Theresa; and Helen, Theresa's childhood friend and Ralph's wife. Divided into five parts, *Typical American* begins with Ralph as a young boy in precommunist China of the late 1930s and concludes sometime in the 1960s in suburban New York. The narration flashes both backward and forward so that the novel's analepses provide the backstory to the Changs' lives in China while the various prolepses not only foreshadow events that comprise the plot of the novel but also project into the futures of the Chang family through the second generation—daughters Callie and Mona. While initially Jen contemplated using the title "In the American Society" for the novel-length narrative of the Chang family, because the story had been mislabeled as "nonfiction" in one of its many republications, Jen's agent Maxine Groffsky suggested the title *Typical American*.

Critics and reviewers have marveled over Jen's artistic talents. While there are those who cannot help but laud her for her abilities in the English language (as if the United States–born and English-speaking Jen would have ever had problems with her native tongue)[4] and those who exclaim that she is "a virtuoso raconteur of the Chinese-American experience,"[5] other reviewers describe a reluctance on nearing the end of the novel, having been swept away in "the intelligence of Gish Jen's prose, its epigrammatic sweep and swiftness."[6]

Part 1, "Sweet Rebellion," tells the tale of how Chang Yifeng came to the United States and became Ralph Chang.[7] Jen's omniscient narrator introduces readers to a six-year-old boy whose ears stick out so badly that he is perpetually trying to flatten them against his head with his hands. He lives with his extended family (a big sister whom he refers to as "Know-It-All" is a particular thorn in his side since his parents are constantly telling him to be more like her) in a small town outside of Shanghai, a place "of dusty shops and rutted roads, of timber and clay" where his father, an ex–government official and a scholar, owns and drives the only car in their rural hamlet.[8] Although Jen begins her novel in China, her concerns clearly lie in the West, as she contains the mounting turmoil and political unrest that fomented at the end of China's "Anti-Japanese War" to a single line within the father's interior musings: "on a fan-cooled veranda, he entertains apocalyptic thoughts of marching armies, a new dynasty, the end of society as they know it."[9] As we know from history, the father's apocalyptic thoughts would indeed come to fruition, but the energy of the narrative lies not in the older, Chinese generation that would experience that cataclysmic upheaval but in the next generation of Chinese who would find themselves turning into Jen's titular "typical Americans."

Yifeng's family's relative wealth enables him to become a scholar like his father and to obtain a private fellowship to pursue graduate study in engineering in the United States, so in 1947 he embarks on a boat that takes him from Shanghai to San Francisco and then on a transcontinental train ride from California to New York. In this way Ralph, like his nineteenth-century emigrant predecessors, leaves China in hopes of a better and more lucrative future in the United States. Yet Ralph's tale is not one of simply hard work and immigrant drive. In Jen's imagining of Ralph's immigrant fable, there are multiple distractions and roadblocks, many that derive through his Prufrock-like inability to act in situations that require action. The first of these distractions comes in the form of the Foreign Student Affairs secretary Cammy, a young white woman who becomes Ralph's first American object of desire and the bestower of his American name, one that Cammy chose from among a roster of her ex-boyfriends. Thus Chang Yifeng is reborn as Ralph Chang. From that initial interaction, Ralph finds himself gravitating to the Foreign Student Affairs Office, especially after, despite all his studious reviewing of math equations on the boat and train coming over to the United States and the time spent studying with his fellow Chinese classmates, his homework is returned to him covered in red marks. Summing up Ralph's infatuation with Cammy, Henry Chao, an older classmate whom everyone refers to as "Old Chao," says, "You wouldn't be in love, Little Chang, if your schoolwork were going better."[10] Indeed, Cammy becomes an object of affection for Ralph that seems easier to decode than his math equations, and with more gratifying results since the small gifts he gives her and favors he does for her are rewarded by her smiles and attention, especially those that entail enlisting his help against the head of the Foreign Student Affairs Office, Mr. Fitt.

When his nascent romance with Cammy fizzles with a chaste kiss to her head (which also coincides with Mr. Fitt firing Cammy over her affair with the dean), Ralph finds a new distraction from his studies in the political events occurring in his homeland: it is 1948, Mao's troops are overtaking the nationalist army, and Ralph's parents have sent a letter asking him to come home. Yet he remains in the United States, along with his fellow Chinese grad students, in protest of the communists but also, in Ralph's case, as a symptom of his own inability to make clear decisions that lead to decisive actions. As Jen has depicted him, Ralph is a comic everyman, a boy whose ears stuck out of his head, a young man with foolish dreams of adventure and success in America, and a graduate student who finds himself unable to move forward in his studies and unable to return home to the turmoil of China.

Ralph's fears over the fate of his parents lead to sleepless nights, which lead him to sleepwalk through his life until he has let his visa expire. Because of his romantic flirtation with Cammy, he avoids seeking help from Mr. Fitt, even when he receives numerous notices from the Foreign Student Affairs Office.

On the advice of his thesis adviser, Professor Pinkus, Ralph decides to lie low and avoid being seen around the university. He takes a job in Chinatown at an underground livestock slaughterhouse because as a native Mandarin speaker he cannot communicate with the Cantonese-speaking owners and patrons of New York City's Chinatown, and this job does not require talking. Slowly but steadily his paranoia over his expired visa has Ralph moving from apartment to apartment each time someone calls his landlord or landlady looking for him, resulting in his moving away from his Chinese friends and his former university life. For a brief moment it seems as if Ralph's visa troubles will be resolved through Pinkus, when he becomes the new head of the department. Ralph goes to visit him; Pinkus says he will try to help; and Ralph, in a misguided sense of gratitude, begins to stalk Pinkus and his family, only to have Pinkus catch him in the act and accuse him of being a sneak and a liar. Briefly contemplating suicide, Ralph ultimately lacks the ability to act on his depression and instead finds himself walking in the winter snow, where on a park bench, miraculously, he is reunited with his "Know-It-All" big sister, Theresa.

While the themes in this first part may seem to be dark and dire—paranoia, suicidal thoughts, depression, political upheaval, visa issues, and threats of deportation—Jen does not depict Ralph or any of her other characters as wretched and despairing. Even after Ralph's lowest moment, when he had a meat cleaver in his hand and thought of killing himself in front of Pinkus's house, he wakes up the next morning to his landlord telling him about a phone call, and instantly he is propelled into survival mode, driven by his paranoia to move yet again and find another apartment. In explaining his curious lethargy, Jen does not resort to morose imagery; instead, to describe the passage of time involving Ralph's inactivity, she uses a confectionary analogy of cake batter: "his days and nights marbled together as though so much vanilla batter, so much chocolate, cut into each other with a knife."[11] Jen is also a master ironist, and the phone calls that Ralph had been dodging for months were actually from Theresa, who, newly arrived in New York, was looking for her younger brother. Thus what propelled Ralph into a state of panic and paranoia, these phone calls, became the life line he grasped onto when his sister finally found him slumped over on that snowy park bench.

Even the reunion scene between Theresa and Ralph is made comic in Jen's hands, as Ralph, in his amazement and ecstasy over seeing his big sister, knocks her to the ground, where she twists her ankle, so that they end up crying and hugging and flagging down a cab to take them to the emergency room, enacting a screwball comedy scene based on familial rather than romantic rescue. Upon Theresa's reunion with Ralph, the omniscient narrator fills in her background story, using analepses to flash back to her life in China and how she came to

New York. While she is mentioned only briefly in the first chapter as Ralph's big sister, whom he refers to as *Bai Xiao* or Know-It-All, a girl who attends Catholic school (which is how she received her English name Theresa) and plays softball, after she finds Ralph she is given her own chapter, "Theresa." There the narrator explains that Theresa is not a typical Chinese girl with feminine traits to entice marriageable young men. Described as smart but homely like her father, at five feet, seven inches tall (over three inches taller than Ralph) she is considered a "giantess" who "strolled when she walked, sometimes with her hands in her pockets."[12] When a suitable suitor is found for her and he requests a prewedding meeting, her mother tells the matchmaker that Theresa will walk by a park gate with a pink parasol and wearing shoes a size too small (in order to make her feet appear dainty). As a result Theresa stumbles painfully across a park in the August heat, only to discover in the end that her would-be fiancé had run off with his father's concubine months before.

As with her depiction of Ralph, Jen uses this anecdote of Theresa's failed courtship not to mock her but to poke fun at the Chinese traditions that force her into this situation. The novel sends up both American and Chinese traditions and conventions, always treating the characters with affection in their various foibles and flawed states of humanity. Jen's omniscient narrator's voice throughout the parasol park scene is wry but tender, putting us in the head of Theresa as she takes one painful step after another across the park gate, only finally to answer the practical call of her body's discomfort by using the parasol as a cane to stagger over to a stand of trees where she can rest in the shade: "Brave, she folded her parasol, hobbled off to the right, leaving the path. She did not look back to the gate, but only forward, toward the peeling sycamores."[13] In this depiction of Theresa, Jen creates a strong female character who is sensitive to family loyalties but also has a sense of her own self worth and preservation. Such preservation eventually leads her to become the companion to the daughter of close family friends, a girl named Hailan whom she renames Helen, after Helen of Troy and out of similarity to her friend's Chinese name.

The final chapter of part 1, "The Deliverance, Continued," sets the scene for the themes, plot, and characters (along with their virtues and flaws) for the remainder of the novel, as the events of Ralph and Theresa's miraculous reunion are recounted by Theresa to Ralph and Helen's future daughters, Callie and Mona, as a prolepsis in some undisclosed future period. In this flash forward we also learn the fate of a friend of Ralph's, Little Lou, who killed himself, as Ralph learns in the Chinese papers. The inclusion of Little Lou's tragic end is a reminder to Ralph and to readers that his fate could have been the same were it not for the intervention of his sister, who became the means of his emotional and physical salvation in more ways than one. Theresa introduces Ralph to her roommate, Helen, who becomes Ralph's new object of affection, this time one who reminds him most poignantly of home through the meals she prepares. Her dishes are so exquisitely evocative of Ralph's childhood that eating her food "inflamed more than abated his homesickness"; so much do they remind him of his family's meals that "his stomach fairly ached with the resemblance, even as his mouth thrilled."[14] He proposes to her after she perfects chicken and fish dishes, and just like that, Ralph has gone from being alone and destitute to embraced by a sister and a wife. Theresa and Helen solve all of Ralph's problems: they find him a job that does not require paperwork; they feed him; and they find a new apartment where all three of them can live together. When it is clear that the communists have taken hold of China, Ralph finds his visa problems solved as he, like a number of other Chinese students stranded in the United States, is granted immunity and sent back to school to complete his Ph.D. training. The chapter and section end with a blurry wedding photo of Ralph, Helen, and Theresa, which they dub "The Mystery of the Trinity"; whether they are able to remain a trinity will be explored in the chapters and sections to come.[15]

Part 2, "The House Holds," opens with another series of analepses, this time looking back on Helen's life in China and her first few months in the United States. Described as a delicate girl, whose twin sister died in childbirth, Helen is doted on by her parents and siblings, "blessed by just enough lingering, sometimes serious illness, to win her much fuss."[16] With the threat of communists taking over the country, she is sent away with Theresa to study in the United States. Initially she is reluctant to eat anything other than Chinese food, or as the omniscient narrator tells us, Helen "was not at home enough, though, even to fall ill." Eventually she acclimates to the United States, learning the language by distinguishing among "interest," "interested," and "interesting"; saying "red, white, and blue" rather than "blue, white, and red"; and marrying Ralph in recognition "that it was time to make herself as at home in her exile as she could."[17] Yet Helen's real transformation occurs not through marriage but through labor. While in Shanghai, due to her illnesses, her gender, and her family's class status, Helen always had servants or family to perform the most basic of tasks for her. In the one-room tenement apartment that she shares with Ralph and Theresa, Helen learns that "working was enjoyable. Effort, result," so that not only is she cooking for the first time and sewing and repairing household items, but she even manages to fix the building's boiler when their super is nowhere to be found, simply by reading the manual and getting the fuel refilled.[18] Helen's ingenuity prompts Theresa to marvel at her, speculating, "What different kinds of intelligence there were in the world! Who was to say which mattered most? One couldn't say, couldn't begin to say, although this much was certain—what mattered in China was not necessarily what mattered here."[19]

This theme, of adjusting to life in the United States and recognizing that their identities in China, their skills sets, were not necessarily going to be the same as in the United States, forms the crux of part 2. It is here that the title of the novel first makes its way into the narrative, as Ralph, Theresa, and Helen find themselves complaining about their American neighbors and their American and distinctly un-Chinese values and behaviors, beginning a recitation of the curiosities, slights, and strangeness of U.S. culture and society with the mantra "typical American," believing themselves immune to the disease of unruly American behavior since they are well-mannered Chinese: "They were sure, of course, that they wouldn't 'become wild' here in America, where there was 'no one to control them.' Yet they were more sure still as they shook their heads over a clerk who short-changed them ('typical American no morals!'). Over a neighbor who snapped his key in his door lock ('typical American use-brute-force!'). Or what about that other neighbor's kid, who claimed the opposite of a Democrat to be a pelican? ('Peckin?' said Ralph. 'A kind of bird,' explained Theresa; then he laughed too. 'Typical American just-dumb!') They discovered stories everywhere."[20]

This shared slogan, while used to highlight cultural and national differences, ones in which the new immigrants can feel a sense of superiority over their ignorant neighbors, is also a survival tactic. In part 3 the omniscient narrator shares an analepsis describing Ralph, Theresa, and Helen and their newly discovered passion for that all-American of sports: baseball. However, the one time they attended a game, "people had called them names and told them to go back to their laundry. They in turn had sat impassive as the scoreboard. Rooting in their hearts, they said later. Anyway, they preferred to stay home and watch."[21] While hurtling racist and bigoted epithets is a "typical American" thing to do, by this point in the narrative the Changs, by Theresa's coaching, have decided that these "typical Americans" are just like them—and indeed the rest of the novel illustrates just how typically American the three Chinese immigrants will become.

While initially the three Changs operate as a single unit in harmony, eventually their differences from one another grow: Ralph and Helen find themselves trying to adjust to being a couple, with all the newly attendant excitement that their physical and sexual coupling brings but also with the strife of arguments and disagreements that beset husbands and wives. Ralph's childhood jealousy of Theresa rears up when she not only is accepted into medical school but also has received a full scholarship—this during a time when Ralph finds his progress toward his Ph.D. stalled and his old habits of indecision and inactivity returning. As Helen gains a sense of her own autonomy and intelligence, one that Theresa recognizes as valuable for its difference from the book learning that she (in medical school) and Ralph (in his engineering program) have developed, Helen finds herself branching outside of the Chang enclave and making friends with other Chinese American immigrant women, particularly Janis Chao, the wife of Ralph's former classmate Old Chao.

Although Janis is figured as a minor character in terms of how fleshed out and developed (or underdeveloped) she is, she is also a catalyst for change in the novel, as through her (and the people she introduces them to) the Changs will have their own lives forever altered. Sensing the tension in their home, Theresa tells Helen that she is thinking of marrying. She has already defused Ralph's jealousy by lying to him and telling him that her scholarship was revoked unexpectedly, which then led to Ralph restarting his research, seemingly buoyed by his sister's reversal of fortune. Helen enlists Janis's help in finding a husband for Theresa, and Janis offers up her Chinese American landlord, Grover Ding, a man so assimilated that he speaks neither Cantonese nor Mandarin and does not know which province his family comes from in China since their arrival to the United States happened generations ago. He is also described as "a handsome, burly, breezy man, about [Ralph's] height, with large teeth, one of them gold, and a powerful jaw."[22] Winking at the visibly pregnant Helen (a wink that will foreshadow future events), Grover behaves badly, first ignoring everyone at the dinner table and then leaving to make phone calls, only to return to the table to take up conversation by mocking his host, Old Chao. This behavior, while turning the Chaos, Helen, and Theresa against him, only seems to enrapture Ralph, "who, head tilted, mouth slack, looked for all the world like someone in love."[23]

Indeed it is Ralph and Grover who end up literally running away together when Grover borrows (or more accurately steals) Old Chao's car under the pretext of wanting to admire it, driving out of the city and into the suburbs and finally stopping at a roadside diner that Grover happens to own. Cars as symbols of deliverance and destruction will be a thematic element that Jen will return to in the novel's climactic moments. At the diner Grover and Ralph order everything off the all-American menu and indulge in various forms of wantonness, from overeating to Grover's seduction of the waitress in the kitchen, which Ralph, politely keeping his distance in the dining room, listens to in wonderment: "From the kitchen came the sound of pots thrown to the floor. *Cronng.* Dishes smashing—*ack! ackk! asssh!* Then laughter. What were they doing that they laughed as they did it? He and Helen never laughed."[24] Ralph's curiosity and comparison of his life with Grover's extend from the sexual to the financial, as he becomes seduced by Grover's talk of how he got his lucky break and became a millionaire and that "in America, anything is possible."[25] In Grover, Ralph finds the inspiration he needs to become an "imaginer"— a buzzword he latches onto after his dissertation adviser gives him a copy of *The Power of Positive Thinking*. Looking for a role model on which he could imagine his future successful self, Ralph becomes enamored with Grover—his talk of lucky breaks, riches, and most importantly confidence, decisiveness, and assurance, all qualities lacking in Ralph's current life.

Yet upon returning to the reality of his run-down tenement apartment, with a concerned and angry pregnant wife and a worried and humiliated jilted sister, Ralph expresses contrition and eventually gives up his dreams to be mentored by Grover, especially when his numerous phone calls to Grover go unanswered. Instead, as a dutiful father-to-be of their first daughter, Callie, Ralph concentrates on finishing his dissertation, "Crack Stress of Airplane Bodies by Computer Analysis," which he completes after the birth of their second daughter, Mona.[26] Part 2 ends with all three Changs accomplishing their personal milestones: Helen births two babies; Ralph graduates with his Ph.D.; and Theresa becomes a medical doctor. With their new degrees and children in hand, the family members move upward and onward into a more spacious apartment and a new chapter in their lives.

Part 3 is aptly titled "This New Life" as the five Changs, or "Chang-kees," as they have dubbed themselves after their beloved Yankees, are discovering the twin American dreams of upward mobility and reinvention. They have taken their naturalization tests and have become American citizens, but their cultural citizenship is described by the narrator through the many ways they are adapting to and adopting the customs of their new homeland: they celebrate Christmas as well as the Chinese new year; they watch baseball and attend performances at Radio City Music Hall; and all three of the adult Changs find themselves thinking in both Chinese and English, slipping fluidly and fluently from one to the other. They also end up buying a car and a house in Westchester, completing the transition from newly arrived urban immigrants to assimilating suburban Americans.

As Jen noted in an interview, "People think you set foot in America and you become American instantly. For the characters in my book, it takes a while to become American and it's not so much becoming a citizen that makes them feel American, it's something like buying a house."[27] The suburban house, which is the primary object of Helen's desire, represents their Americanization. Tellingly, Jen does not have her characters living in Chinatown, either before or after their move to the suburbs, and curiously their friendships do not seem to involve large groups of fellow Chinese immigrants. Helen's only close friend besides Theresa seems to be Janis Chao, and the only other people she socializes with in the suburbs are her American neighbors: Arthur Smith, who discusses lawn care with her, and three women with whom she plays bridge, none of whom have Asian surnames. Indeed the move to the suburbs evokes imagery reminiscent of the final paragraphs in *The Great Gatsby,* as the Changs compare their old urban existence with this new suburban dream: "The deeper their former life sank in the black muck of ignorance, the higher their present life seemed to spring. So bright it shone, so radiant with truth and discovery! It was as if the land they had been living in had turned out to be no land at all, but a mere offshore island, a featureless mound of muddy scrub and barnacle-laced rock, barely big enough for a hospital, an engineering school. Whereas this New World—now this was a continent. A paradise, they agreed."[28] While this intertextual reference may not be intended by the author, Jen's novel is most thoroughly an American creation rather than one that evokes ethnic stereotypes of Chinatown ghettoes and cultural clashes. Noting that Jen's narrative signals a departure from other Asian immigrant narratives in its relocation from Chinatown to the suburbs, the literary critic Betsy Huang observes that "Gish Jen rewrites the script that has long dominated Chinese-American immigrant fiction, and complicates firm notions of Chinese and American identities that have been staple elements of the script."[29] While the Changs may be waxing rhapsodic over their new life in the suburbs, as Huang aptly notes, theirs is not a simple story of assimilation or disillusionment in American society.

This middle segment of the novel does not feature as many plot developments and major events, either political or personal. Instead the choices and decisions that the Changs make are of a more domestic nature—squabbles to settle between Mona and Callie, arguments between Helen and Ralph over mowing the lawn, and Theresa convincing Ralph that she should chip in on the mortgage payments for their new house since she will be living with them for the foreseeable future, her marital desires having dissolved with one disastrous nondate with Grover Ding. Yet there are two tensions explored in this section: Ralph's march toward tenure and Theresa's relationship with Old Chao. That Ralph may not get tenure is invoked during a chance meeting in the hospital emergency room between Theresa and Old Chao, who has hemorrhoids, as Theresa diagnoses upon reading the medical chart before realizing that it is Old Chao she will be seeing: "Why did people come into the emergency room for hemorrhoids? [*sic*] but of course they did, for sunburn too, and gas."[30]

From this first odd and comic encounter, Theresa and Old Chao will continue to talk and develop "a small intimacy. Who would have predicted the larger ones to follow?"[31] As the omniscient narrator foreshadows, the initial platonic lunches, in which Chao confesses his fears over Ralph's tenure prospects, turn into more meaningful encounters. Chao, who as head of the engineering

CHAPTER 3

Mona in the Promised Land
Switching and Choosing One's Identity

Although often believed to be the sequel to *Typical American, Mona in the Promised Land* (1996) can be read as a stand-alone novel that does not require familiarity with her previous narrative, though readers who are already acquainted with the Chang family—Ralph, Helen, and their two daughters, Callie and Mona—will be pleased to see that the family has remained intact and that the girls have grown beyond their elementary-school-aged selves. Like her first novel, her second was born out of a short story, "What Means Switch?" (1990), originally printed in the *Atlantic Monthly* and reproduced as the first chapter in *Mona in the Promised Land*. After the reactions that Jen received from publishing *Typical American* in which she was lauded as the representative voice of Chinese Americans and/or Asian Americans while also being lumped together with her fellow authors of Asian ancestry who published novels in 1991, Jen decided to upend people's expectations about the kind of writer she is and the kind of material she writes.[1] Jen has explained that she had jotted down notes on index cards for future stories: "I looked at one of the cards and it said, 'Mona turns Jewish.' And I thought 'Oy! Can't write that,' and I laughed. Then I paid attention. The uncomfortable laughter told me that I'd hit a nerve."[2] In writing *Mona in the Promised Land,* Jen has succeeded in hitting a larger national nerve in the United States about our attitudes on race, religion, the freedom to choose for ourselves who we want to be, and the costs of those choices. As Jen noted about her second novel, "I've tried to contribute to the process of boundary crossing, to painting pictures that are a little less black and white—a little more complicated."[3]

Reviewers and scholars of *Mona in the Promised Land* have rightfully paid attention to themes of gender and ethnic identity and, most telling, to the limits of self-identification and to questions of ethnic essentialism and cross-racial alliances, themes that make this novel a rich text to analyze for what it says about issues of identity in the waning days of the modern civil rights era of the United States. Almost all the reviews about *Mona* laud Jen for her sophomore effort. Writing for the *New York Times Book Review,* Jacqueline Carey observed that "*Mona in the Promised Land* has a wide-ranging exuberance that's unusual in what is still—to its credit—a realistic novel. Ms. Jen doesn't sacrifice her characters to satire. And her story can take the broad view even while it focuses on smaller, more personal matters because she works in so many voices and because she includes so many perfectly timed set pieces."[4] Valerie Miner noted in a review for the *Nation,* "The strength and grace of Jen's novel is in her rueful wisdom about being an immigrant family's daughter."[5] The *Los Angeles Times Book Review* critic Richard Eder paid Jen the compliment of likening her to Hemingway in her creation of a distinctively American voice for her protagonist: "Mona is telling an American story imbued with a Chinese sensibility, one for which the new what-should-be never quite eclipses the old what-is. And—her greatest achievement—Jen has devised a diction for Mona to tell it in. Hemingway invented his rhythms to create his particular American world. Jen invents a percussive tempo, a series of brusquely energetic leaps and breaks that, without being anything but idiomatic, create an extended particular world where dim sum is as American as apple pie."[6]

However, not all reviewers could see beyond the surface of the author's face and race. The *Washington Post Book World* critic Jonathan Yardley first reduced the plot and theme of *Typical American* to those of a standard assimilation story in the Changs' desire to become "typical Americans" and then reduced the uniqueness of the narrative by likening its content to Amy Tan's *The Joy Luck Club* and other Asian American books written in the same period, since they are "all dealing, in their different ways, with much the same subject."[7] When Yardley finally got around to discussing Jen's second novel, he wondered if it is not perhaps simply autobiography since *Mona in the Promised Land* "fairly trumpets its origins in the author's own experience," implying that Jen's craft as a writer is reducible to that of a diarist.[8] The remainder of the review was condescending toward Jen as a contemporary American writer and to her subject matter. Yardley chided Jen for the immature and inauthentic voice she created for her teenage protagonist Mona Chang. More egregiously he read *Mona* as a novel that has its second-generation daughters, Callie and Mona, grappling with "the tensions between China and America," thereby misreading the novel as one of simplistic and stereotypical immigrant conflict rather than the more nuanced vision of American life presented in the novel—a vision of life for Chinese Americans that is not simply about the clash of ethnic cultures.[9]

Thankfully scholars who have written about Jen's second novel have been more accurate in their evaluations of Jen's work and how it fits into late twentieth-century American literature. Indeed, *Mona in the Promised Land* has enjoyed popularity in literary criticism among Jewish American, Asian American, and contemporary American literary scholars. Perhaps the predominance of articles and book chapters that look at *Mona in the Promised Land* can be credited to its unique subject matter: a Chinese American Catholic converting to Judaism. Perhaps it has received wide attention due to its historical backdrop: the multicultural atmosphere of the end of the civil rights movement; the sexual and gender empowerment of women; and the general atmosphere of activism and freedom of the late 1960s and early 1970s. Or perhaps a theme of the novel, of negotiating between an identity you choose for yourself versus the one you were born into and that society prescribes for you, resonates with many academics interested in contemporary ethnic American literature. The literary critic Andrew Furman believes that "*Mona in the Promised Land* is not so much about the Jewish American rise to socio-economic and cultural confidence nor is it about the Chinese-Americans' parallel journey as the 'New Jews' (3). Rather than merely trace these cultural evolutions, Jen goes after decidedly bigger fish as she engages the paradigm shift regarding the immigrant ethos precipitated in large part by the multicultural enthusiasms of the 1960s that continue apace today."[10]

For Jeffrey Partridge, whose essay on *Mona* is included in the edited collection *Complicating Constructions: Race, Ethnicity, and Hybridity in American Texts,* the novel is first and foremost an American construction: "What characterizes Americanness in the novel is not what one becomes, but the very act of becoming. In other words, 'becoming,' the novel suggests, is the hallmark of being American."[11] Cathy Schlund-Vials, in her monograph *Modeling Citizenship: Jewish and Asian American Writing,* offers a reading of *Mona* alongside Mary Antin's *The Promised Land,* thus putting into conversation Gish Jen's late twentieth-century American novel about a girl's struggle with her Chinese American Jewish identity alongside an early twentieth-century American novel about an immigrant girl's struggle to negotiate between her Jewish and American selves. As Schlund-Vials notes, "If Mary Antin's literary intent was to 'write herself' into the larger U.S. narrative, Jen attempts, through Mona, to fictionally imagine an alternative U.S. narrative wherein 'switches' are in the end recognized."[12]

Divided into three parts, each containing five chapters, and with an epilogue that takes readers into the far future, *Mona in the Promised Land,* as its title suggests, focuses on the youngest Chang family member, the eponymous heroine of this comic bildungsroman. Similar to *Typical American, Mona in the Promised Land* is narrated with a heterodiegetic narrator, an all-knowing and all-seeing storyteller, who continues to use the occasional analepsis and prolepsis to flash backward and forward to the lives of the Changs and their friends. However, where the first novel bounced from Ralph to Theresa to Helen's actions, inner musings, and perspective, in this follow-up to the Chang saga the omniscient narrator is almost entirely restricted to Mona's sights, sounds, thoughts, and feelings, with occasional glimpses into the behaviors and inner lives of her family members and friends. The central theme in *Mona* is the ability of one to choose, or in Jen's language "switch," identities since the central tension that the plot revolves around is Mona's decision to convert to Judaism, a choice she makes that proves contentious with her Chinese immigrant parents. Added to the heightened tensions of her already fraught teen years is the backdrop of the early 1970s and the political fomenting (civil rights, anti–Vietnam war protests, the sexual revolution and women's rights) that Jen amusingly describes.

The paratextual epigraphs that Jen includes at the start of her narrative alert readers to the themes of the novel and the myriad cultural influences that have shaped her as a writer. Quotes from the Latino author Richard Rodriguez, the Japanese American poet and memoirist David Mura, Ovid, and a selection from the I Ching all describe how people change their affiliations. Rodriguez's quote talks about him becoming Chinese, and Mura's talks about how he knew more Yiddish than Japanese. The I Ching considers the person who can change tribal allegiances as "Supreme good fortune," especially since such change is beyond the realm of ordinary men.[13] As the Ovid epigraph says, ". . . all things change. The cosmos itself is flux and motion."[14] Thus when readers enter part 1, they encounter movement, first in the form of a decision that Ralph and Helen are trying to make: "The parents slide the question back and forth like a cup of ginseng neither one wants to drink," and next in the actual relocation that the Chang family undertakes to Scarshill, a more affluent suburb than the one they are leaving behind—as their realtor says, "'Moneyed! Many delis!' In other words, rich and Jewish."[15]

Beyond the theme of movement (also found in the title of the first chapter, "Mona Gets Flipped"), the opening paragraph also announces an interest in subverting notions of what it means to be a typical Chinese or Chinese American. Where in her first novel Jen defiantly declares, "It's an American story"[16] and then proceeds to describe the life of a small Chinese boy in a rural village outside Shanghai, Jen begins her second by proclaiming, "There they are, nice Chinese family—father, mother, two born-here girls."[17] However, those who expect to find a traditional tale about Chinese family values quickly learn that the omniscient narrator has other ideas in mind because the metaphorical gin-seng tea that Ralph and Helen slide back and forth is replaced by their desire for something all-American: "what they really want is a milk shake (chocolate), and to go with it a house in Scarshill."[18] By the first page the narrator is telling us that it is 1968 and that the Changs' upward mobility is reminiscent of an older ethnic enclave since they, like their fellow Asian brethren in America, have become "the New Jews . . . a model minority and Great American Success."[19] Yet because we know this is a comedy, what follows in the remaining pages will not be a paean to American assimilation and upward mobility; instead Jen charts the comic foibles and follies of Mona and her family as they adjust to being not just "New Jews" but in Mona's case a real Jewish Chinese American through her conversion to Judaism.

As the title of chapter 1 prophetically announces, Mona will indeed get flipped at the end of this chapter, literally and eventually religiously, ethnically, and politically as well. Once the Chang clan (minus Aunt Theresa) has moved to Scarshill (which is the fictional version of Scarsdale, the actual New York suburb where the actual author Gish Jen grew up), Mona finds that she has moved up in the world, both in terms of her class standing and in her social sphere. As the only Chinese American (besides her sister, Callie) in the school, she finds herself an exotic object of attention and interest, and she milks that interest for all the popularity points she can get. She tells her classmates that she knows karate, knows how to get pregnant by just drinking tea, and knows Chinese—all of which are either outright lies or gross exaggerations; her flu-ency in Shanghaiese boils down to the phrases "Ji-nu" and "Shee-veh," which translate to "Soy sauce. Rice Gruel."[20]

Her authentic Asian act is challenged when an even more authentically Asian student arrives in the form of Sherman Matsumoto, a boy whose Japa-nese parents are temporarily in the United States on business and whose Eng-lish is, initially, only slightly better than Mona's Chinese. Because Sherman's mother has asked the school to place him with other "Orientals," Mona is as-signed as his guide to American high school life, and he follows her from class to class, eats lunch with her, and traipses around town with her to department stores and the bagel shop.[21] He and Mona also discuss issues of nationality and identity. When Sherman asks her if she is American, Mona replies, "Sure I'm American. . . . Everybody who's born here is American, and also some people who convert from what they were before. You could become Ameri-can."[22] Going further, Mona foreshadows her own impending conversion when she speculates, "I could become Jewish, if I wanted to. I'd just have to switch, that's all."[23]

While Mona makes a change of religion and ethnicity sound like a simple matter of turning on a lightbulb, the reality of such a conversion, and its ramifications, is certainly much more complicated than simply switching, as will be illustrated later in the novel. In this opening chapter, however, Mona is still firmly entrenched as a Chinese American girl who finds herself falling for a Japanese boy. Their nascent romance, however, never goes much further than holding hands and a few furtive kisses on the day Sherman has to leave Scarshill to return to Japan. When he suggests that she can move to Japan and switch to being Japanese, she responds, "*I think you should switch. The way you do everything is weird.*"[24] It is at this point that Mona gets flipped by the judo-proficient Sherman, who confirms their breakup after he has returned to Japan by writing and telling her, "*You will never be Japanese.*"[25] Mona's reluctance to turn Japanese and Sherman's affirmation that Japaneseness will always elude her seem to be more about the vagaries of their teen romance than based on any real knowledge of Japanese customs and practices; certainly Sherman as her sole interlocutor for all things Japanese is not a reliable barometer for how well she would or would not adapt to being Japanese. So the first chapter ends with Mona's thwarted first romance with Sherman at the age of thirteen. Yet despite the brevity of their relationship, Sherman's presence will reverberate in significant ways as a vital plot point in the remaining narrative.

One way that Sherman Matsumoto becomes significant, thematically, is in his racial similarity to and yet ethnic and cultural difference from Mona. By introducing Sherman in the first chapter of the novel, Jen makes a point of showing that not all Asians are the same. Indeed while Sherman's mother might have desired Sherman to make a connection with a fellow "Oriental," the reality is that he and Mona share few similarities in terms of their ethnic and national affiliations. Their relationship develops more due to their differences than any racial solidarity; thus Jen subverts readers' expectations of seeing all Asians as the same by detailing the crucial differences between someone, for example Mona, who is born and raised as an American of Asian descent versus a figure, for example Sherman, born in Asia and temporarily sojourning in the United States.

After Sherman's departure, the rest of part 1 focuses on Mona's teenage life. Chapter 2, "Her Life More Generally," provides background on the rest of the nuclear Chang family. We learn how Ralph and Helen purchased the pancake house, a joint investment made with Janis, the former wife of Old Chao. We learn about Callie's embarrassment about working at said pancake house and some minor skirmishes between two cooks, resulting in a punch in the face and the firing of an employee over some missing minute steaks. In addition we learn what happened to Aunt Theresa. There are two specific allusions to the events of *Typical American* besides the reference that the omniscient narrator makes to the Chicken Palace debacle as "the complicated subject of another whole book."[26] The first reference occurs when Helen tells her daughters, "Your aunt Theresa, she really suffered";[27] and the second occurs when we learn what happened to Theresa in the aftermath of her coma, namely that she has relocated to California along with Uncle Henry, who has divorced Janis but remains unmarried to Theresa, a mild scandal that the narrator reports along with the rumor that Theresa might be on the beach "in a two-piece bathing suit and sometimes less."[28] That Theresa's beach attire is noted before her unmarried-but-living-together state signals a change in attitude by Ralph and Helen, perhaps brought about by the near tragic events at the end of *Typical American* and perhaps as evidence that the subjects that matter in this sequel squarely rest with the eponymous Mona and her coming-of-age.

The last three chapters of part 1 describe Mona's conversion to Judaism, which begins first as a way for her to be like her many Jewish friends, since "pretty soon Mona's tagged along to so many temple car washes and food drives, not to say weekend conclavettes, that she's been named official mascot of the Temple Youth Group."[29] Her transition from virtual to actual Jewish convert occurs slowly but surely throughout the chapters. Mona is questioned about her intentions by Rabbi Horowitz, who is more conservative than his "Hasid turned rock star" appearance suggests and who becomes Mona's spiritual adviser, pushing her to see that her desire to convert may be partly out of teenage rebellion and presciently telling her, "*The more Jewish you become, the more Chinese you'll be.*"[30] Although Mona acknowledges that being like her friends and unlike her parents may play a part in her conversion calculations, the sense of inquiry and social justice that is evident in the Temple Youth Group and her own nascent notions of Judaism spur her desire to become Jewish.

While Rabbi Horowitz comes to recognize Mona's conversion wishes as truly felt, Mona's parents are not so sanguine about their youngest daughter's decision to become Jewish, particularly since Mona had received Catholic Church confirmation at the age of sixteen, which she received along with her driver's permit, as seen in the opening of chapter 3. While religion is never emphasized in *Typical American,* there are references to Theresa and Helen attending a convent school in Shanghai and to Ralph's attendance in church at their behest. Though neither Helen nor Ralph seems overly invested in Callie and Mona being Catholic, Mona's conversion rattles Helen in particular, who sees it as a sign of Mona's distancing herself from her parents' culture and influence and becoming more and more like the typical Americans whom she and the other adult Changs decried in Jen's first novel.

However, for Mona, her conversion is completely in keeping with her nationality and the spirit of freedom to be found in the United States. As she tells
Helen, "American means being whatever you want, and I happened to pick
being Jewish."[31] Just as Mona foreshadowed in her conversation with Sherman, if she decided she wanted to switch and become Jewish, she could. Yet
her conversion is not a simple matter of exchange; she does not cease to be
part of her Chinese American family or to be seen as an Asian anomaly amid
her white Jewish friends. Instead, Mona continues to navigate her new Jewish
self through the parameters of teenage life where she remains a double outlier:
the only Jew in her Catholic Chinese family; the only Chinese American in her
Temple Youth Group; and the only Asian American among her high school
peers.

While Mona negotiates her outsider status, it is not depicted by the narrator as an alienating experience, at least not more so than the normal ways in
which teenagers experience alienation. Alongside her various minority statuses
Mona is also coping with the standard expressions of adolescent tension and
angst: the cliques that emerge; the couplings of her friends; and the crushes
she experiences, as both object and subject. For example, there is Seth Mandel, who eyes her as a source of romantic interest since he believes her to be
an iconoclast along the lines of Yoko Ono, an antiestablishment independent
thinker. After Mona sets him straight, he turns his attention to her best friend,
Barbara, who ends up breaking things off with him after a pregnancy scare is
thankfully only a scare. But while Seth and Barbara are pairing off in the broom
closet of the Temple Hot Line, Mona finds herself receiving hotline phone calls
from a mysterious Japanese-identified caller who may or may not be her ex-
beau, Sherman Matsumoto, and who hangs up on Mona before she is able to
establish whether he has indeed returned to the United States and whether they
will ever have a future.

Barbara, believing the would-be Sherman to be a ruse invented by her in-
veterate crush, Andy Kaplan, interrupts as Mona is talking to Sherman, only
to have him once again tell her, "You will never be Japanese."[32] A contrite
Barbara apologizes to Mona by giving her the keys to her van, which she lends
to Mona while she is away on vacation. However, Seth also has a set of keys, so
that Mona and Seth end up sharing the van. Mona finds herself attacked after
thwarting an attempted robbery of said van. Thinking that the robber is actually Seth, Mona covers his eyes in order to surprise him, only to find that the
surprise is on her when the masked assailant pins her to the ground. Thankfully
Seth comes to her rescue on his bike and knocks the attacker to the ground.
Part 1 comes to a close with the rescued Mona being revived by "Seth Mandel,
her avenging angel, bicycle pump in hand."[33]

While part 2 has no title, this mid-section of the novel could well be called "Mona's Teenage Experiment Phase," as Mona undergoes several new summertime experiences, including a romantic relationship with her rescuer, Seth Mandel, whose postattack comforting of her leads to an intimacy that has Mona feeling "that she owns a whole self inside the self that she knows, someone sharing her skin."[34] Mona will find that this new whole self is not simply a sexual self but also a self brought to life through the climate of social justice activism of the early 1970s. Through Seth, Mona finds herself contemplating issues of racial justice, class warfare, and sexual freedom, often as they pass around a joint, since Mona is also engaging in some light drug experimentation in the form of pot smoking, which Jen uses in keeping with the times as well as to accent Mona's high school persona. However, Mona finds her newfound interest in activism at odds with her parents' beliefs, especially Helen, who takes offense at a white woman petitioning for a sliding-fee women's health clinic, telling Mona, "We are not Negroes. You hear me? Why should we work so hard—so people can talk to us about birth control for free?"[35] Thus, Mona finds herself caught between her friends' idealism and fervor for racial equity and social justice and her Chinese immigrant parents' rhetoric of hard work and wanting to distance themselves from a population they believe is ranked at the bottom of the U.S. social hierarchy.

Yet this division is not a clear-cut binary between the bad immigrant conservative parents and the progressive Jewish youths. Jen craftily demonstrates Seth's idealist hypocrisy when he calls Ralph a "capital oppressor" who exploits his workers.[36] This is after Seth has been hired to work at the pancake house along with Barbara; their employment happens not out of economic necessity but to keep Mona company, since she needs to contribute to the family's income by hostessing during the summer. While her friends have families who have liquid assets and who vacation at the shore, Mona's family does not enjoy these types of luxuries. Yet Seth, in particular, has a myopic vision of class oppression. In Jen's depiction, Seth is a likable but short-sighted young man, a self-proclaimed antiestablishment rebel who is living in a teepee. Yet much like that American iconoclast Thoreau, Seth is similarly dependent on others for his rebellion, as the teepee is pitched in his parents' yard, where he is able to run an electrical extension cord to his teepee and where he can avail himself of a refrigerator full of food.[37] His partaking in his parents' upper-middle-class comforts does not stop him from criticizing their bourgeois life, as he is particularly censorious toward his stepmother, Bea, whose charity work he dismisses as a form of her guilt and status seeking. When Seth is similarly dismissive of his new boss and his girlfriend's father, Mona sets him straight about the realities of her parents' finances in comparison to his own: "We're not like you. We don't have investments. We don't read the *Wall Street Journal*. I've never even seen a stock certificate,"[38] after which Seth apologizes by saying, "Excuse me for confusing your class status."[39] While he does not acknowledge his hypocrisy, he does learn to see that Mona's Chinese immigrant parents face a different class and racial reality than that of his Jewish American parents.

Taking a break from her friends and family, Mona ventures to a Rhode Island resort where her sister, Callie, is working. Also working there is Callie's Harvard roommate, Naomi, an African American "Renaissance woman"[40] who practices yoga, listens to jazz, cooks tea-smoked duck, and teaches Mona to see herself as a fellow colored person: "*You are yellow. A yellow person. A yellow girl,*" a revelation for Mona, who had understood that she was not white but "had never thought of herself as colored before."[41] What Mona learns from spending the week with Callie and Naomi is to spy on the white patrons of the summer resort, ones who ask the plaid-clad waitresses (who are attired in kilts and polo shirts) which part of Scotland they are from, "to which Callie answers, the Far Eastern part; and Naomi, that she's not actually from Scotland. She is, she says, from deepest, darkest Wales."[42] The spying will aid the Harvard students' research project about race, class, and leisure, or as Naomi sums up, "What they're talking about is status."[43]

Indeed status is another central theme, along with identity, in this novel. At the end of chapter 6, "Into the Teepee" (the first chapter of part 2), the omniscient narrator offers readers a prolepsis into the future Mona's life in which she goes to an art exhibit on Chinese portraiture: "Members of society were depicted in terms of their activities and their clothes, which was to say their rank. For these clothes were not about self-expression; these were closer to uniforms. And that was what mattered—not these people's inner selves, but their place in society."[44] Discussing these paintings with a friend who believes that the people in these frames would have chosen to portray themselves differently, as more distinctive and individual, Mona disagrees: "For she understood what mattered most to the people in the pictures as if it still mattered most to her: not that the world would know them for themselves—they would never dare to dream of any such thing—but only that they might know that they belonged, and where."[45] Through this flash forward Jen, vis-à-vis her omniscient narrator, conveys the search for place and identity that the teenage Mona strives for in the mid-section of this narrative. While the adult Mona has moved past concerns of status, "what still matter[s] most" to the adolescent Mona is knowing that she has a group she belongs to—a social standing and status that is legible to her and others.

This search for community leads Mona initially to spy for Naomi and Callie, but when she encounters a classmate, Eloise Ingle, whom Mona had previously regarded as a potential rival in her best-friend standing with Barbara Gugelstein, Mona finds that her initial attempts to pretend to be friendly with Eloise for covert purposes turn into an actual friendship once Mona learns more about Eloise and sees beyond her own exterior trappings of upper-class wealth and social status. All of this culminates in Mona attending a comically rendered dinner as a guest of the Ingles. Mona, ordering an enormous amount of food since it is the kind of resort where meals are all-inclusive, learns from her Waspy hosts that "to order doubles is another thing that *simply is not done*."[46] After a particularly difficult struggle with a lobster in which Mona squirts juice all over Naomi, their server, Mrs. Ingle asks Mona where she is from (not being satisfied with Mona's initial response, "The same town as you"), to which Mona then replies, "Ah . . . Deepest Darkest China."[47] Mona's cheeky answer signals that she has absorbed both the politics and the humor of Naomi and Callie, seeing herself aligned with them as part of their community of colored women. But her newfound friendship with Eloise shows that she can look beyond exteriors too. She offers sanctuary to Eloise when Eloise impulsively decides to run away from home (or rather to leave her family's suite at the resort), a short-lived experiment that ends when Eloise's father comes for her in the servants' quarters of the resort, where Naomi and Callie are housed and where Mona is temporarily staying.

The other central drama of part 2 occurs when one of the African American cooks, Alfred, is thrown out of his home by his wife, Charlene. Trying to live out the activism of their time and teenage idealism, Barbara offers him the room over the garage in her new home (which the narrator describes as more of a palatial estate), where she is staying with her cousin Evie, who has been brought from Minneapolis to keep her company since Barbara has decided not to vacation with her parents at their summer home on the shore. Alfred is soon surreptitiously coming and going from the Gugelstein estate through tunnels that run from the wine cellar to the woods behind their subdivision, part of the original Underground Railroad, or so Barbara is told. Although Barbara originally keeps Alfred's presence in the house a secret from Evie, who is holed up in her room developing photos most of the time, not only does Evie eventually learn about Alfred, but Alfred and Evie end up becoming a couple. Alfred invites over his friends Luther, Ray, Big Benson, and Professor Estimator, black men who talk openly about issues of race and class and who along with the Jewish teens form an interracial mod squad that they dub "Camp Gugelstein" (which is also the name of chapter 10, the last in part 2). For a few weeks the Jewish teenagers and Alfred and his friends gather together to play games (checkers, chess, billiards, badminton); to practice yoga and Buddhist meditation; and to talk across the lines of race, about hair, particularly the nuances of African American hair styles, and about current events, such as the war in Viet Nam, civil rights and integration, or about more prosaic issues such as car repair. Swept up in the interracial unity of the group, "Seth buys himself a dashiki like Luther's—his camp shirt."[48] The differences among these disparate people are also swept away with this simplistically hopeful assessment: "Here too is a gang who loomed up like strangers not long ago. Now, though, they are friends, plain and simple—already!"[49]

The em dash in the previous quote along with the optimistic exclamation mark attached to the adverb "already" make this an ironic statement in light of the next paragraph, which announces in a simple declarative sentence, "A flask is missing."[50] Where earlier the interracial harmony of this group seemed to be a simple matter of finding commonalities that turn strangers into friends, a harmony accomplished "already!," lulling readers into a sense of how easily racial unity can be won, with the declaration of missing property, racial lines will be drawn between the Jewish teens and the black men. Indeed, Camp Gugelstein's racial utopia quickly disintegrates when Barbara confronts the black men over her family's missing silver flask. Previously the friends had sat in a circle holding hands, hands that, focalized through Mona, are described not through color but through touch: "There are warm palms, cool palms, firm grips, loose; and attached to them such an amazing array of humanity."[51] However, when Barbara questions Alfred and his friends, "she makes everyone sit on a folding chair."[52] Although everyone except Barbara sits in the folding chairs, only the black men are questioned over the missing flask, a point not lost on Alfred and his friends, as Luther declares, "A lot of racist bullshit coming down here."[53] The men, who refuse to dignify Barbara's accusation, leave, only to return the next day to move Alfred out of Barbara's house and into a place of his own because "he doesn't have to stay with some white folk like a charity case," at which point Camp Gugelstein has officially come to an end.[54]

With the end of the group come other finales. One is an end to Seth's idealism in black-white interracial harmony, which can also be read as Jen's commentary on the idealism of youth and the complexities of interracial race relations. Both Mona and Barbara are more circumspect about the disintegration of Camp Gugelstein, in part believing that "their purpose was to help Alfred back on his own feet, and they did. They wanted him to be independent of them, and he is."[55] However, Seth has a harder time with the dissolution of the group, acknowledging his naïveté in believing that their interracial experiment could continue but nonetheless lamenting that "they considered me a racist bastard, and I considered them my friends."[56] In this statement, which Seth says in a moment of self-pity, Jen encapsulates the tensions inherent in interracial friendships and relationships. Unequal power dynamics invaded the group when Barbara, a young white Jewish teenager, accused the black men of stealing her family's flask. Through that accusation, and Mona, Seth, and Evie's silent complicity with allowing Barbara to accuse the men, Seth went from being a friend to the mod squad to another white man who suspects black men of committing crime. His naïveté lies not just in believing that their interracial group could last but also in not seeing the way that his privilege as a white man and his lack of recognition of that privilege contributed to the end of his friendships.

Although Alfred initially stands by Evie, staying with her even as his friends ride off in a righteous wave of black pride, eventually their relationship folds under the pressure of racial tensions, with Alfred declaring, "All she wanted was to be fucked by a black man" and Evie asserting, "All he wanted was a chick even whiter than Charlene"—both statements reducing the others to stereotypes.[57] Along with the disintegration of these various interracial relationships comes the close of summer, as the last chapter ends with Labor Day weekend. It also ends with Mona deciding that she is ready to have sex with Seth, and so she avails herself of the "new almost free clinic" that has opened in their neighborhood, allowing her a final experimental moment in the sexual entanglements she undergoes with Seth in his teepee.[58] As part 2 comes to a close, so does Mona's summer of experimentation as she begins her senior year of high school.

At the conclusion of part 2 Evie, in her depression over her breakup with Alfred, has left incriminating photos of them in bed together, which Barbara's mother finds (having returned home from her summer vacation at the shore), along with the pictorial evidence of Camp Gugelstein and Alfred's temporary residence in the Gugelstein home. Part 3 opens with chapter 11, "The Fall Begins," and the consequences of that photographic discovery: Evie's departure back to Minneapolis and Alfred's firing from the pancake house. Mona's parents, learning about Alfred's relationship with Evie and Mona's part in his unauthorized stay at the Gugelstein home, fire him to save face with Barbara's parents, believing him to be an extension of themselves, as Helen tells Mona, "How do you think we feel? Our cook act like that."[59] But Helen's decision to fire Alfred also stems from her disapproval of his relationship with Evie: "'He is our cook,' says Helen again. 'And that girl, she is white.'"[60] While Mona tries to challenge her mother about her racism, she also tries to give her a silver lining to this incident by telling her that at least she was not sleeping with Alfred. Yet Helen finds this to be such an abhorrent idea that she tells Mona, "You do that, I would kill myself," thus foreshadowing the strong reaction that Helen might have to finding her own daughter in an interracial sexual dalliance.

However, Helen does not need to worry about Mona just now since Mona has decided to break up with Seth, telling him that he has wanted to mold her into someone in his own image so "that somehow her experiment has turned into his experiment."[61] Admitting that he did not mean to pull a Henry Higgins on her, Seth declares his love for Mona, and when she does not relent, he tries to win her back, pursuing her at the pancake house until he is fired. He then resorts to writing love letters to her and, in an homage to an obscure line in Chekhov's play *The Cherry Orchard,* jumps off the roof of the one-story ranch house; he tells his friends to tell Mona "that he hoped she got the reference to a well-known Russian play involving a cherry orchard. Luckily, he was unhurt."[62] When Mona still does not react to his attempts to make amends to her, he decides to attend college and move away from Scarshill, having determined to join the rest of his peer group in this educational journey. But he leaves behind an enigmatic message for Mona on the back of a fortune cookie: "In Seth's minute scrawl, it reads: Watch for the return of a most mannerly fellow."[63]

With Seth's departure comes the arrival of Sherman, who surprises Mona at her high school, appearing to be so changed that she hardly recognizes him: "Gone the baby-fat upholstery, and the poky pink flush. . . . As for the old hole in his left eyebrow, that has grown over without a trace. . . . How much Sherman has grown! He is taller than Seth easily."[64] Although Sherman abruptly leaves after an initial greeting, he calls her later that afternoon and, being less reticent than before, discloses more details about his life since Mona last saw him. While previously Sherman had wanted Mona to move to Japan and become Japanese, now he tells her that since his family has spent so much time living abroad, they do not feel at home in Japan any longer, and he now considers himself Hawaiian since he has lived there for some time. Additionally Sherman has traded judo for baseball, switching his allegiances to being 100 percent American. From the renewal of their phone conversations comes a newfound relationship in which Mona finds herself opening up to Sherman about her family and the pressure she feels "to be their everything." She explains, "Jews believe in the here and now; Catholics believe in heaven; the Chinese believe in the next generation."[65] Mona, in discussing these issues with her old flame, is trying to decipher how to navigate her life as a formerly Catholic and now a Jewish Chinese American girl maturing into womanhood.

Unfortunately tensions between Mona and her parents escalate in the next chapter, "A Stay of Execution," when Alfred files a discrimination lawsuit again the Changs for his termination. Seeking counsel from someone they trust, the Changs enlist the aid of Aunt Theresa, who arrives from California bearing flower leis and a straw bag full of figs, lemons, and other bountiful homegrown produce. She has also arrived a changed woman from the skinny and homely spinster who finally found love at the end of *Typical American*. This new Aunt Theresa "is wiry and tan and sweetly befreckled . . . wearing her brown hair all loose now" and sports "blue jeans like a hippie, only new-looking and fresh-pressed."[66] Listening patiently to Helen and Ralph's version of events, Theresa wisely observes that there is no discrimination since they would have fired their Chinese head cook Cedric for the same behavior as Alfred's. However, their relief is short-lived as Mona confesses to her family that she has revealed to Barbara, Seth, Alfred, and Luther the conversations her parents have had about whom they can trust for promotion, namely that Cedric received his promotion as head cook because he was Chinese, which means that Alfred was never considered for promotion due to his not being Chinese, if not due to the fact of being black.

Presciently predicting a time when Mona may need to seek refuge from the parental storm that is forming over this revelation, Theresa offers an invitation: "You are welcome to come to California anytime. Anytime you like, you can come make yourself at home."[67] Indeed the question of where Mona can find herself at home is a central theme in part 3. One of the reasons she breaks up with Seth comes from feeling not quite at home with him, and her discussions with Sherman center on where she belongs—where she feels most at home. Her current home life is indeed stormy. Initially Helen and Ralph receive the news of Mona's confession with equanimity, placing the blame on themselves for abdicating their parenting responsibilities, as Helen affirms: "No more typical American parents. . . . No more let the kids run wild. From now on we are Chinese parents."[68] Yet once Theresa leaves, Helen takes out her anger on Mona, admonishing her for telling her friends about their family's private issues and for calling her parents racist, an act that Helen regards as the actions of a disloyal and disrespectful child: "Parents are racist, parents are not racist, even parents are communist, a daughter has no business talk like that. You talk like that is like slap your own mother in the face!"[69] As if to punctuate her point, Helen slaps Mona when her youngest daughter tells her that she no longer wants to live in the Chang home. When Mona tells her mother that she is not Callie and cannot be treated this way, Helen slaps her a second time and says, "You think you are so smart, you think you know everything. But let me tell you something: Once you leave this house you can never come back." With that Helen turns away and chapter 12 comes to an end.[70]

Chapter 13, "Mona's Life as Callie," finds Mona in Grand Central Station full of endless possibilities. Amid her anxiety over running away she recognizes another feeling, "something opening within herself, big as the train station, streaming with sappy light."[71] Anticipation rather than foreboding marks Mona's running-away experience, and she is aided in her newfound feeling of bigness by a fortunate encounter with Seth's philanthropic stepmother, Bea, who listens sympathetically to Mona and gives her a hundred dollars and the reassurance that she will call her parents to let them know she is safe. Mona then departs for the college tour that her parents found superfluous, traveling to Yale, Brown, the University of Massachusetts at Amherst, and Smith College before finally ending up in Cambridge at her sister's dorm suite at Harvard. Discovering that Callie has left for a trip to New York City, Mona assumes her sister's life by wearing her clothes, using her toothbrush, and attending her classes. When her parents call, they are unable to tell that they are speaking to Mona rather than Callie, which is how Mona learns that her sister has told them that she has run away to be with Aunt Theresa. The next phone call that Mona-as-Callie receives is from Sherman, who also, initially, cannot tell that he is speaking to the wrong Chang daughter. However, when he does eventually venture that the similarity between Callie and Mona is uncanny, enough to have him suspect that he is speaking with Mona rather than Callie, she hangs up on him, a reversal of their hotline phone calls in which it was the cagey Sherman who abruptly ended conversations by hanging up on Mona.

Callie returns from her New York City excursion, where she and Naomi had tried to pitch their Rhode Island resort project as a book proposal. However, the editor had been more interested in Naomi's story than Callie's since, as Callie explains to Mona, "Naomi's experience has an import ours just doesn't. After all, blacks are the majority minority."[72] Here Jen slyly inserts a wink into the text since readers are, in fact, reading a book about a minority-minority. This insertion speaks to the ways that Asian Americans were not seen as a group worthy of storytelling in the early 1970s, although it could also be a sly wink to the publication of Maxine Hong Kingston's *Woman Warrior*, published by Random House in 1975, which is approximately when the action of part 3 takes place. Undaunted from the rejection, especially since Callie is told by the editor, "People are interested in China," she tells Mona that despite the fact that she has never been to China, she thinks that "it would be cool to write a book" and plans to wear a Chinese dress when she is next in New York.[73] In the 1970s Callie cannot envision getting a book published about Chinese Americans without resorting to self-exoticization and promoting an affiliation with China that she does not have, which is precisely the point that Gish Jen is trying to make about the marketing forces that drive Asian Americans writers to this kind of Orientalizing. Fortunately for Jen's readers, it is no longer the 1970s, and instead we get to read about actual Chinese Americans navigating their lives in the United States, ones who, like Mona, are undergoing teenage conflicts with an added Jewish twist.

With Callie's return comes Mona's disclosure to her parents that she is not with Auntie Theresa but is instead with Callie at Harvard. While her parents are relieved that she is safe, they are also angry at her disobedience, and Helen hangs up on Mona when Mona asks her if she wants her to come back. Helen does want her to return but cannot admit it for that will force her to lose face. Mona next enlists the help of Callie and Naomi in getting Sherman to meet her face-to-face, and so Callie lies to him when he calls looking for Mona, telling him that Mona is on her deathbed and that they are sitting shiva, mispronouncing it as "shee-veh, which means rice gruel in Shanghainese."[74] When Sherman arrives at the end of chapter 13, he reveals himself to be, as in chapter 14's apt title, "A Most Mannerly Fellow," none other than Mona's most recent ex-beau: "Mona yanks open the ever-sticky door to welcome who else but Seth Mandel. In voice he is Sherman Matsumoto. In person he is the person he always was, only thinner."[75] As Seth and Mona become reacquainted, he recounts the evolution of Sherman Matsumoto from real Japanese student to disembodied voice. The initial calls that Mona fielded while working on the Temple hotline were designed by classmate Andy Kaplan as a joke. However, he stopped because, as Seth relates, "He worried it was mean. Also it was getting too weird. It was weird how much he liked having an alter ego," thus once again evoking the novel's interest in issues of identity, albeit in the form of a disguise rather than the search for one's authentic self.[76]

Yet the idea of what an authentic self is is complicated. As Seth explains the Sherman ruse more to Mona, he tells her that when he took over the role from Andy, he was coached by him on the voice, which he could not get right, so Sherman had to become someone from Hawaii. He also discloses that the Sherman whom Mona thought she met was actually a Japanese American from Hawaii who was on exchange at a local high school, and his last name was Matsumoto, even if his first name was Trevor rather than Sherman. In getting into the role of his alter ego, Seth immersed himself in Japanese culture by sleeping on a futon, eating with chopsticks, and buying tatami mats for his teepee. In the process he tells Mona that "he's begun to feel, actually, sort of Japanese. Or at least that the Japanese manner corresponds to something in him," again returning to the theme of the novel: that what you are inside may or may not be commensurate with the way you were raised or the family into which you were born.[77]

Although Mona is reluctant to forgive Seth, they eventually reconcile, to the point where they are found in flagrante delicto by Ralph and Helen, who have journeyed to Cambridge to retrieve their wayward daughter. Instead of a reunion between parents and child, the Changs encounter a naked Seth, who hides his genitals with one of Callie's textbooks while Mona hides behind him covered in bedsheets. Retreating from this scene, Helen and Ralph leave the newly recoupled Seth and Mona, as Mona watches them cross Harvard Yard dejected over the revelation of their daughter in such a compromising position. Deciding that Mona should lie low until her parents' shock wears off, Seth and Mona decamp to the newly vacant Gugelstein estate, compliments of Barbara, whose family has left the old palatial home (leased when Mr. Gugelstein received his raise) for Barbara's smaller childhood home (which luckily had not been sold when Mr. Gugelstein learned that he had been fired from his Wall Street firm). While hiding out at the old Gugelstein homestead, Mona and Seth discover the real culprit behind the missing silver flask: Fernando, the old line cook who had been fired due to his punching of Cedric and his theft of a box of steaks. Fernando is also suspected of being Mona's attacker from the end of part 1, with Seth surmising that he has been stalking Mona for the last year, which is how he knew to find them hiding out in the ex-Gugelstein manse.

In the final chapter of part 3, "Discoveries," Mona and Seth seek out Alfred in order to give him the flask and obtain his forgiveness. As they sit down in Alfred's apartment, the three former friends resume their old conversational patterns, catching each other up on their lives and the lives of the other mod squad members. Alfred then reveals that he has been in touch with Evie, perhaps hinting at an impending reconciliation, but the greatest disclosure he provides is to tell Mona that he has decided to drop the lawsuit against the Changs. Mona rushes home to share this good news with her parents, picturing her mother's relief: "She imagines the in-suck of her mother's body as it straightens—a little lighter, a little younger—and this makes Mona feel similarly floaty."[78] Entering the house for the first time since her fight with Helen, Mona encounters her home as at once familiar and unfamiliar, seeing, as if for the first time, the jumbled nature of the Chang kitchen with its cuckoo clock and cabinets "crammed full of cans and bottles, rolls of things, years of stuff."[79] In surmising about the kind of kitchen Mona will have one day, the omniscient narrator wonders if Mona will choose a kitchen "that bespoke law and order and recipes you can write down" or whether "her kitchen will be exactly like this. A bargain basement, hardly elegant, hardly a place where you could execute with efficiency your culinary intentions; but where you might start out making one thing, only to end up, miraculously, with a most delicious *dish du jour*."[80] Through this extended domestic analogy, the narrator returns once again to the larger themes of the novel: whether Mona will choose a future self in opposition to those of her parents or whether her familial patterns will influence her not to be exactly like them but to be the kind of person who is free to reinvent herself and, like the cooking metaphor, can start out intending to be one thing only to end up being something else, something that is good and of this present moment.[81]

Calling out for her mother, Mona encounters the startling vision of an unkempt Helen wearing her bathrobe in the middle of the day, her hair disheveled and her face without her glasses, giving her the appearance of advanced age. Following her mother to her parents' bedroom, Mona exclaims to Helen, "Alfred is dropping the suit! We talked to him!" to which Helen responds, "What are you talking about, talked to Alfred? . . . And who is this *we*?"[82] In emphasizing that last pronoun, questioning its very validity, Helen reinforces her former angry edicts to Mona about killing herself if Mona were ever involved in an interracial sexual dalliance and in telling her that if she runs away from home, she can never return. By questioning Mona's "we," Helen emphasizes that she acknowledges neither Mona's coupling with Seth nor her existence as her daughter, and so the narrative of Mona Chang's coming-of-age ends with Mona being forced to grow up and to leave her parents' house. The final paragraph concludes with the narrator focalizing the scene first through Helen and then through Mona's perspective: "Helen returns to her bedroom: and this time she doesn't even close the door, she doesn't have to. For it's as if this is what she's seen with her glasses off, operating on inner sight—that this disturbance can be trusted to leave by herself. Finally she's big enough not to need to be told."[83]

The story of Mona's teenage life may end with chapter 15, but the final word on Mona, along with her assorted friends and family, comes in the novel's epilogue. In these final pages we flash forward to an adult Mona who is getting married, officially, to Seth Mandel at Aunt Theresa's California beach home. In the lead-up to the wedding ceremony, we learn that despite a few detours in their relationship, Mona and Seth have been living together long enough to be considered a common-law couple by the government; they have also created Io, their one-year-old daughter, whom they were going to name Helen if Mona's mother had shown up at the hospital. However, the rift begun at the end of part 3 has continued into Mona's adulthood, though Ralph has eventually reconciled with his youngest daughter and Seth, even getting to the point where he brags about his pseudo son-in-law to friends, telling them, "*My son-in-law, he eats everything. . . . Even the leftovers he eats. Right out of the refrigerator. He does not even use the microwave oven. . . .* And Ralph's friends are impressed. *. . . Not even Chinese, but he eats everything.*"[84]

The omniscient narrator also informs us of what happened to several of Mona's friends: Evie and Alfred are now married with three children; Naomi has become an author; Barbara and Andy Kaplan have been married and remarried twice, their reunions made difficult due to their professional careers working for the airlines; and big sister Callie has become the doctor her parents always wanted her to be, complete with a husband, a home, and two children. Callie has also changed her name to Kailan and identifies as Asian American, leaving Ralph and Helen to "shake their heads. Better to turn Jewish than Asian American, that's their opinion these days,"[85] since they wonder, "What in the world is an Asian American? . . . And how can she lump herself together with the Japanese?"[86] With tongue firmly planted in cheek, Jen raises one of the thorny issues of identifying as Asian American, namely the flattening of pan-ethnic differences into a monolithic racial community, one in which the histories of Chinese-Japanese conflict are rendered superfluous in the face of Asian American pride, which Callie lists as the reason for her Chinese name change.

The narrator saves the most dramatic reversal for the last page of the novel, as the doorbell rings, announcing the long-awaited but never-anticipated arrival of Mona's mother. The mother and daughter reunion leaves both Helen and Mona crying, with little Io acting as a witness to this happy-tearful scene. In the spirit of a true comedy that ends in a marriage, Jen leaves readers with two unions: the impending marriage of Seth and Mona; and the joining together of Helen and Mona. The omniscient narrator observes that "the way she's crying, anyone would think that Helen is the person Mona's taking in sickness or in health—is it really her mother, so tiny? The way Mona's crying, anyone would think that she's being taken too—finally!—for better or worse. *Until death do us part,* she thinks, and rushes forward."[87] As the exclamation announces, finally Helen accepts Mona for who she is, for better or worse, in sickness or in health. Finally Mona can be acknowledged by her mother for the woman she has become rather than the disappointment Helen has lived with. The novel ends with this marriage of mother and daughter in mutual agreement to love and cherish each other for the limited time they have (since the narrative hints at Helen's heart ailments), so Jen closes her coming-of-age narrative after the grown-up Mona has finally come into her own through her mother's embrace.

department at an unnamed university has hired his would-be friend Ralph, explains to Theresa that space is the area engineers are zeroing in on. It is the late 1950s, and Ralph's attention to mechanics seems a mistake in the Cold War race into space. Yet despite Theresa's mild inquiries and attempts to steer Ralph into a more secure position in his department, Ralph stubbornly sticks with his research plan, which eventually does win him tenure since, as Old Chao tells him, "*With everyone going over to space, we really did need someone in straight mechanics.*"[32] As readers will observe, the preceding line is rendered in italics, which is Jen's way of signaling that her characters are speaking Chinese to one another rather than English. Choosing this textual form of difference to signify linguistic difference, Jen, through her omniscient narrator, allows us inside the minds of the Chinese characters and their speech without relying on clunky Orientalist ornamentation. This allows readers to see that these characters converse in both English and Chinese and to experience that fluidity as the characters do.

Although Old Chao initially seems to pursue a friendship with Theresa as a way of helping Ralph, larger intimacies do follow, until eventually Theresa finds that the platonic friendship has turned into a torrid affair. The chaste lunches that they previously enjoyed are now surreptitious occasions for their lusty pairing. Theresa eventually discloses the friendship to Ralph and Helen (Ralph had previously caught sight of Old Chao having lunch with a thin Chinese woman who was not his wife in an abandoned corner of the chemistry department; not initially suspecting his sister, he is shocked at Old Chao's behavior). Upon finding out that his sister is Old Chao's lunchtime companion, both Ralph and Helen censure her, leading Theresa finally to succumb to the physical desires she had previously held in check, so that by the end of "This New Life," Theresa has certainly found a newly awakened sexual life with Old Chao.

Part 4, "Structural Weakening," announces both a rift and a shift in the Chang household. While Ralph would seem to have the perfect life—tenure, two healthy daughters, a reliable wife, and a house in the suburbs—part 4 opens with his discontent over the status quo of teaching and research that Ralph finds is his everyday existence and a prolepsis in which the narrator shows us a future Ralph who is a "chastened man, an older man" reflecting back on a single decision he made that would irrevocably lead to the disastrous events chronicled in the remainder of the novel.[33] While in the first half of the narrative Ralph is depicted as a Prufrock-like figure with an inability to act decisively, the second half of the novel features a reckless Ralph whose dogmatic decisions lead to his downfall. Bored with his job, Ralph impulsively calls Grover Ding, whose number he recalls from memory, having dialed it over and over again years before. This time, however, Grover not only picks up but also remembers Ralph, inviting him to join him for dinner and in a business opportunity that seems too good to be true, and of course turns out to be too good to be true.

Smooth-talking Grover sells Ralph a take-out chicken joint, with a lengthy explanation (which Ralph recounts to Helen and Theresa) of how Ralph will then sell the store back to Grover under the table and that Ralph will eventually buy it back from him through the lucrative proceeds from the restaurant, but the name on the deed throughout all these transactions will be Ralph's. In making his pitch to Ralph, Grover tells Ralph that this business "could be the start of a real success story. This could be the start of a self-made man."[34] Revisiting his earlier dreams of being an imaginer, Ralph succumbs to the promise of a rags-to-riches story in which he will achieve the American dream of instant wealth and the respect and confidence that accompany such a lifestyle of a so-called self-made man. In this way Ralph is becoming more and more like the typical Americans he had earlier decried, caring more about the trappings of wealth and status than the idea of contentment and stability through hard work.

While Helen is initially hesitant and Theresa outright critical of Grover's business scheme, Ralph soothes the former and dismisses the latter. Indeed from the moment of Theresa's revelation of a relationship with Old Chao, Ralph has been scornful toward her, deriding her in front of the girls and answering her skepticism by telling her, "You have nothing to say," indicating that her moral lapse leaves her without any authority to question Ralph.[35] So much has Theresa's standing in the family eroded that soon she feels displaced as the fried chicken take-out place takes off, calming Helen's fears of financial ruin and replacing it with the material goods she has coveted for their house—in particular a blue love seat that will soon be the staging ground for Helen's own moral lapse into extramarital romance with none other than their would-be benefactor Grover, or as the girls learn to call him, "Uncle Grover." As their fortunes rise, so does the Changs' affection for Grover, which feels to Theresa in inverse proportion to her own waning status as favorite family member, until one night, with Ralph acting particularly cruel toward his big sister, "a small man making fun," as the omniscient narrator observes, Theresa packs up and moves out.[36]

Into Theresa's absence strides Grover, who cozies up to Helen while Ralph is downstairs in his basement office creating fake receipts on a cash register, which is how their fortunes are able to rise: "Underreporting made all the difference. They weren't rich, but by paying less tax they became respectable."[37] On the blue love seat that Helen bought as a symbol of their middle-class status, she finds herself wooed by Grover, seduced by his talk of her beauty and charmed by his attention, in much the same way that her husband is similarly enraptured by the easy money and success he believes Grover's patronage brings them. In Jen's depiction, Ralph is a man who cannot see the forest for the trees, one who ignores signs of impending storm clouds until he finds himself drenched in his car with the top down. Blind to all but his greed, he ignores the romance happening above him in his living room since he is too busy cooking the books. It is Helen who finally puts an end to the affair through an accurately aimed display of her manicured nails to Grover's groin. It is after his painful departure that Grover agrees to Ralph's idea of increasing year-round business by building a second story onto the take-out place, guaranteeing chicken-eating customers in rain, snow, or sunshine in the newly dubbed Ralph's Chicken Palace.

The phrase "structural weakening" is a metaphor for the state of the Chang household: Theresa's departure to her own apartment; Helen's affair with Grover; and Ralph's ethical lapse in defrauding the government. Yet it also refers to a literal weakening of the newly dubbed Chicken Palace (or Chicken Place, as the sign reads after the "A" falls off with the settling of the building) as cracks in the walls grow larger and longer and seem to symbolize the cracks in Ralph and Helen's marriage and in the formerly united Chang-kees. While business is initially booming in the Chicken Palace, Ralph learns the extent of Grover's perfidy when he grows suspicious of his soon-to-be former friend. Tracking down the previous owner of the take-out place, Ralph discovers the fraud that Grover committed with the original owner and the unusable land that the restaurant sits on, a lot filled with rotting timber into which the two-story building is slowly but steadily settling. With Grover's claim to their house (which they signed over to him in order to get a loan from him to build the second-story addition) and without any legal remedy, Ralph and Helen can do nothing except watch the cracks in the walls and creaks in the building grow while employees quit over unsafe working conditions, until Ralph, unable to ignore a particularly unsettling seismic shudder, orders everyone out of the building as part 4 comes to a close.

The final section, part 5, "A Man to Sit at Supper and Never Eat," opens with the dismantling of the Chicken Palace and the unraveling of Ralph and Helen's marriage, exacerbated by the financial stress due to the lack of income coming into their home and Ralph's trademark torpor. After working together to close the store, Ralph and Helen retreat to their separate spheres. Helen tries to keep their family afloat by looking for work, only to be turned away because "there were still enough women around for the stores to be picky. They could afford to have white women, who spoke English without accents,"[38] ones who would not be asked, "Are you a gook?" by fellow clerks.[39] Ralph, refusing to return to the university, even though Old Chao has held summer school classes for him, instead impulsively gets a puppy, ostensibly for the girls, but the dog (whom he names Grover) becomes the new object of his desire and affection, a new distraction from the financial and emotional debacle in which the Chang family members find themselves. Much like the cracks that formed in the former Chicken Palace, the cracks in the Chang family have disastrous results, as a particularly nasty fight between Helen and Ralph escalates from a thrown hairbrush, to Ralph lunging at Helen, to Helen falling through their second-story bedroom window—a fall that is miraculously broken by overgrown hemlocks and a downward-sloping lawn. This particular detail was originally included in the short story "The Water Faucet Vision," and Jen integrated it into her novel to show just how far the former Chang-kees have fallen—to demonstrate the ways that they have turned into those typical Americans whom they had formerly lamented as being without morals and manners.

Here they are, then, a fractured family, emotionally and literally. Yet this fight does lead Ralph to attempt to make amends by returning to his university teaching assignment and by telling Helen that he will do whatever she wants and needs, which leads to Theresa's return to the Chang household. With Theresa, however, come her two cats, previously named Callie and Mona in honor of the nieces she missed and now renamed Ken and Barbie by the human namesakes. Also with Theresa's arrival comes Old Chao, who has declared his love for Theresa and his willingness to leave Janis and their children. Theresa, however, is ambivalent, and Janis is surprisingly acquiescent with her husband's transfer of affections. The person who has the toughest time adjusting to Old Chao's relationship with Theresa is Ralph, who hides inside the bedroom whenever Old Chao comes to visit. However, he does not protest since his sister's income allows them to keep their home and because his guilt over the fight with Helen that resulted in her flying through the window prevents him from asserting his discomfort.

His contrition, however, is short-lived once he reencounters Grover, who has purchased the woods behind the Changs' house for a development opportunity. Ralph finds Grover on the ridge overlooking his suburban neighborhood, but before he can confront him over his fraudulent business dealings, Grover fuels the suspicions Ralph had been having about Helen's faithfulness (or lack thereof) by broadly hinting at their previous dalliances on the blue love seat. Rushing back to the house, Ralph drags Helen to their car and drives off while screaming at her to tell him what happened between her and Grover.

CHAPTER 4

Who's Irish?

The Short Fiction of Gish Jen

Gish Jen was publishing short fiction even before she received her M.F.A. degree from the Iowa Writers' Workshop in 1983. Although her literary acclaim is often linked to her novels, particularly the first two chronicles of the Chang family, *Typical American* and *Mona in the Promised Land*, her craft as a writer is most in evidence through the compact form of the short story. There she creates an entire world in just a few pages, a world so complete and fully realized that readers may want to know more, but the story is its own concise form of art. Evidence of Jen's brilliance in this genre can be found in the number of times her stories have been reprinted in anthologies and edited collections and featured in *The Best American Short Story* series (to date her work has appeared three times in that prestigious series, most recently in 2013 for her story "The Third Dumpster," and her work "Birthmates" was additionally selected for *Best American Short Stories of the Century*). As just one example of Jen's literary reputation, her story "What Means Switch?" originally published in the *Atlantic Monthly* (1990) and reworked as the first chapter of *Mona in the Promised Land* (1996), has been reprinted fifteen times, for example in the Japanese version of *Esquire* (1990), in the anthology *Growing Up Female* (Penguin, 1993), and in *Coming of Age in America* (W. W. Norton, 1994).[1] Indeed, as "What Means Switch" indicates, Jen often uses her short stories as entry points into her long fiction; the Chang family first came to life in her 1986 short story "In the American Society," and the themes and concerns of her other long fiction are in evidence through her short stories.

In *Who's Irish? Stories* (1999) Jen has assembled a sampling of her strongest work of short fiction. All but two of the eight stories collected in *Who's*

Irish? had been previously published in venues such as *Ploughshares, Nimrod,* the *Southern Review,* and the *New Yorker* (which published the title story the previous year). Most notably the work that would be included in *The Best American Short Stories of the Century,* "Birthmates," is the second story in the collection, followed by the 1988 *Best American Short Story* selection "The Water Faucet Vision." Readers who have been following Jen's literary career will be pleased to see that the Chang family is featured in two of these stories ("The Water Faucet Vision" and "In the American Society"), and many of the themes that Jen explored in her first two novels appear throughout these stories, both old and new, suggesting that Jen has thought deeply about questions of generational conflict ("Who's Irish?"), intrafamily dynamics ("Just Wait"), challenges of immigrant households ("Chin"), the limits of cross-racial solidarity ("Birthmates"), problems of cross-national communication when "returning" to the land of one's ethnic ancestry ("Duncan in China"), and the gender and racial politics of interracial relationships ("House, House, Home").[2] As the *New York Times* book critic Michiko Kakutani observed about this collection, "[Jen] has a keen eye for the incongruities of contemporary life, and in this beautifully articulated new collection of stories, she gives us a gently satiric look at the American Dream and its fallout on those who pursue it. She captures the absurdities and self-indulgences of a country where adjectives like creative are attached to everything from guitar playing to the selection of clothes, but she also captures the wonderful sense of freedom it can confer on individuals who are new to its shores."[3]

In this collection, as in nearly all of the stories she has published, her main characters are "typically American," but in this case they are Asian American, specifically Chinese American in *Who's Irish?*[4] While the issues are often specific to those encountered by Chinese immigrants or their second-generation children, they also delve into universal concerns about the disintegration of a marriage, parent-child interrelations and tensions, and the desire for others to recognize a person for who that person truly is. Most especially, the stories in this collection all focus on the theme of home. Whether Jen portrays the instability of literally finding oneself without a roof over one's head or the more abstract questioning of where one feels most at home, her short fiction grapples with the idea and ideal of home. Asking Jen about the themes in *Who's Irish?,* the critic Rachel Lee queried, "So questions of race and ethnicity overlay these stories, which are also about larger issues of home and exile?," to which Jen affirmed, "That's right."[5]

The teleology of the collection is unclear, since it follows neither a chronological order of publication nor a thematic movement of immigrant to citizen nor a chronology of historical period internal to each story, from the 1960s

Meanwhile, Theresa, coming home to a house with no adults and two hungry nieces, worries about Ralph and Helen. After first feeding the girls, Theresa goes to feed Grover the dog, who, being trained by Ralph to attack her cats (a passive-aggressive act toward Theresa over his disapproval of Old Chao), tries to attack Theresa. In trying to run away from Grover the dog, Theresa ends up fleeing to the open door of the garage just as Ralph wildly veers into the driveway, and he plows into his sister.

Once again members of the Chang family find themselves in the emergency room, but Theresa, unlike Helen, did not have her fall miraculously absorbed by overgrown trees. Instead she lies in a coma, with doctors unsure whether she will ever wake up. To pay for the medical bills, Ralph returns to teaching full time, and the Changs sell their suburban dream home and prepare to move into an apartment. The girls take on more adult roles than their elementary-school-aged selves would normally be subjected to, as Ralph and Helen rely on them to pack up their aunt's bedroom for the impending move, a responsibility they perform lovingly if somberly. It is the strength of her relationship with her nieces that seems to rouse Theresa, as it is their names she says most clearly upon awakening from her comatose state. After Helen calls to tell Ralph that Theresa has opened her eyes and has asked for him, he rushes out into the snow (summer having passed into fall and then winter for the duration of Theresa's inert hospital stay). As he is hailing a cab, he thinks with remorse and shame about the words he will need when seeing his sister, remembering back to their childhood in China when their lives were simpler and their relationship one of shared childhood activities. Yet most interestingly, the image that Jen leaves readers with in the final page of her novel is a memory that Ralph has of the hottest day of the summer. Trying to avoid Old Chao's visit, he had sequestered himself in his bedroom, but he could not help peeking at the vision in his back-yard of Theresa and Old Chao "floating in twin inflatable rafts, in twin blue wading pools of water."[40] Thinking back to this memory "on this, the worst day of the winter," this vision now gives him hope, and the omniscient narrator leaves us with Ralph's wonderment that he did not know that "Theresa owned a bathing suit. An orange one! Old Chao's was gray, a more predictable choice."[41]

This image of Theresa and Chao floating in kiddie pools was an intentional rebuttal to the omniscient narrator's revelation that Ralph, on "the worst day of the winter," comes to the bleak realization that "a man was the sum of his limits; freedom only made him see how much so."[42] When asked about this line in an interview, Jen revealed that while Ralph does think this, it is imme-diately followed by his recollection of this summertime scene of "freedom and possibility," so that the "image is supposed to undercut the statement so that it's not only that. That's one truth, and there's also this other truth. Possibilities despite the limits."[43] Possibilities despite limits resonates as a core theme in Jen's first novel and serves as an apt slogan for her creative output as an Asian American author since she is a writer who is most definitely an American, typical or not.

to the present moment. The collection begins with the title story, "Who's Irish?" (1998), followed by two previously published works, "Birthmates" (1994) and "The Water Faucet Vision" (1987). Next comes one of two original pieces, "Duncan in China," followed by three previously published stories, "Just Wait" (1998), "Chin" (1998), and "In the American Society" (1986). The last story, "House, House, Home," is the other original piece created for this collection, and at seventy-five pages it is also the longest of the eight stories. Yet despite the lack of an obvious rationale for the order of the collection, there does seem to be a thematic logic to beginning with "Who's Irish?" and ending with "House, House, Home." The immigrant mother of the first story could be a relative of the immigrant mother in the last, and the adult Chinese American daughter's perspective lacking in the first story is focalized through the Chinese American daughter of the final piece, so that the stories that bookend this collection provide two different voices and musings from a mother and a daughter who are both trying to understand how they ended up living lives so different from the ones they originally envisioned for themselves. Yet despite this loose connection between the stories that begin and end the collection, readers should feel free to follow an order different from the one provided in the table of contents; indeed for those who want to see the development of Jen's authorial voice, readers should read the pieces in the order in which they were published.

The penultimate tale in *Who's Irish?*, "In the American Society," is the oldest of the stories and the one most reprinted (twenty times). Originally published by the *Southern Review* in 1986, this is the first story in which readers are introduced to the Chang family: Ralph, Helen, Callie, and Mona. Although the homodiegetic narration is told through the voice of Callie, the subject and focus of the story is Ralph Chang. Callie's first-person narrator reflects back on her life from an adult distance, as the opening two sentences tell readers, "When my father took over the pancake house, it was to send my little sister Mona and me to college. We were only in junior high at the time, but my father believed in getting a jump on things."[6] The two central tensions explored in this story are the challenges in operating the pancake house and the Changs' attempt to join their town's country club. In both cases Ralph's actions and opinions form the basis of exploring these tensions and of the story's resolution, even as he is being filtered through the focalization of Callie remembering back on this time in their lives.

As we learn from Callie in the second paragraph, the Changs' investment in the pancake house pays off: "We got rich right away . . . those same hotcakes that could barely withstand the weight of butter and syrup were supporting our family with ease."[7] Their newfound prosperity leads Helen to buy a new car, one that has air-conditioning, and to contemplate joining the town's country club, a luxury that had certain obstacles in terms of a nomination from a club member and Ralph's sartorial compliance, namely in the form of wearing a jacket. Callie explains, "My father had no use for nice clothes, and would wear only ten-year-old shirts, with grease-spotted pants, to show how little he cared what anyone thought."[8] Ralph's indifference to the opinion of others is summed up by Helen: "Your father doesn't believe in joining the American society. . . . He wants to have his own society."[9] Here we have the phrase that forms the title of this story as well as the central conflict: Ralph's eschewing of the norms of the society he now finds himself in versus the rest of his family's desire to be in "the American society" and claim all the markers of status it entails, such as joining a country club. This conflict, between Ralph's wishes versus those of his wife and daughters, is seemingly insurmountable since, as the narrator says, "to embrace what my father embraced was to love him; and to embrace something else was to betray him."[10] Acculturation to U.S. norms and society is thus couched as a betrayal; yet as the story demonstrates, Ralph cannot sustain a society of his own since he, his family, the staff at the pancake house, and his neighbors are all living in the United States.

In particular it is Ralph's myopia to the lives of his workers that forms one of the main narrative threads. Callie relates his old-fashioned paternalistic attitude toward his staff, such as giving them money to bail out a relative from jail; however, Ralph then expects them to do extra work outside of the pancake house, for example gardening at the Chang home or repairing broken radiators. When Booker, a Taiwanese worker, appears and offers to do anything needed, Ralph hires him, despite Booker's admission that his student visa has lapsed and his assurance that "I do not think, anyway, that it is against law to hire me, only to be me"—a prophetic statement that turns out to be true when a disgruntled ex-employee whom has Ralph fired calls the Immigration and Naturalization Service to report Booker and his friend Cedric, of similarly expired visa status.[11] Ralph tries to help them, first discovering "that Booker was right. It was illegal for aliens to work, but it wasn't to hire them" and then deciding to sponsor both of "his boys," which is how he refers to Booker and Cedric, for permanent residency after he has bailed them out of jail.[12] Although Booker and Cedric are initially grateful for Ralph's largesse, in the end they leave a note for Ralph along with $140 to pay him back for the bail money, telling him that they have decided to run away rather than go to trial since *"People saying the law in America is fears like dragon."*[13]

Dejected from his attempts to help manage this situation, one that reminded him of his own precarious visa status when he first came to the United States, and contrite over hiring illegal aliens since he did not tell Helen about their status until after their arrest, Ralph becomes open to Helen's suggestion of joining the country club. Although their initial application is rejected, despite the recommendation of Mrs. Lardner, the mother of Mona's friend Annie, they are invited to a bon voyage party at the club for a friend of Mrs. Lardner's who is going to Greece. As with the events surrounding the pancake house, the party is rendered through Callie's observant eyes and remembrances of the conversations of this bygone time. Helen insists that for the event Ralph purchase a suit, which is too large for him but which the salesgirl tacks up temporarily since the tailor cannot alter the coat until after the party; Ralph decides to keep the price tag on in case he wants to return this ill-fitting item. He initially finds himself enjoying the festivities at the country club. But when a drunken club member accosts him, first asking him if he will translate some Chinese characters on a handkerchief and then accusing Ralph of crashing the party, Ralph's tepid enthusiasm for country club life evaporates. Mrs. Lardner subdues the drunken member, who tries to apologize to Ralph, insisting that he take his polo shirt since Ralph seems overdressed amid the Bermuda shorts and wrap skirts of the club members. Although Ralph attempts to shrug him off, the drunken man takes off Ralph's jacket and embarrasses him by announcing the discounted price to the partygoers and telling Ralph to take off his shirt so that he can now wear the man's polo. When the man threatens to drop the jacket into the swimming pool, Ralph throws first the polo shirt and then his jacket into the pool and then storms out of the party with the rest of the Changs.

The story ends without reflection from the adult Callie; instead it is narrated as if these events had just happened rather than being told from the point of view of distant time. We do not have Callie telling us about lessons learned or the consequences of this aborted attempt to join the club. Instead the image that Jen leaves us with is a united Chang family, with Mona complimenting her father for standing up to the drunken man and Helen apologizing for creating the circumstances that led to this swimming pool scene. What we also find in this last scene is Jen's trademark humor, as Ralph informs his family that his keys were in the jacket now sitting on the bottom of the pool. Helen suggests that they walk to the pancake house and stay there until the party is over, at which point they can enlist the aid of Mrs. Lardner in retrieving the jacket. Ralph tells the girls that they "are good swimmers," intimating that they will be the ones to dive for the jacket. The last line of the story shows that the Changs are all in unison: "Then his shirt started moving again, and we trooped up the hill after it, into the dark."[14] With this last line, Callie shows that they have not betrayed Ralph; the Changs make up a society of their own, a home of their own in this American society.

Although the invocation of the pancake house signals the similar terrain found in *Mona in the Promised Land,* both this story and the other one that features the Chang family, "The Water Faucet Vision," do and do not line up with the events and circumstances detailed in Jen's first two novels. Instead both stories should be seen as small-scale models for the larger fictional buildings into which the book-length narratives developed. Originally published in *Nimrod,* "The Water Faucet Vision" (1987) was selected for the 1988 *Best American Short Stories* edition by the guest editor Mark Helprin. Like "In the American Society," this tale, which is the third story in *Who's Irish?,* is narrated by an older Callie looking back on tumultuous events that occurred when she was in the fifth grade. "The Water Faucet Vision" moves between the temporal modes of the distant past, when Callie and Mona are elementary-school-aged, and a present in which the adult Callie tells us that "it's been four months since my mother died."[15] The title alludes to a vision that the devout Callie had about the return of malachite beads that she lost in a sewer drain, but the story is about the adult Callie's grief over the death of her mother and the memory she has of a particularly bad fight between her parents, one that ended with Helen sailing through her bedroom window and falling miraculously into a group of untrimmed hemlock trees, which is also a scene that Jen refined and included in *Typical American.* Her parents' marital strife is mirrored in the family of her best friend, Patty Creamer, whose father abandoned their family. Patty told Callie, "He went on a boat to Rio Deniro. . . . He said he would rather look at water than at my mom's fat face. He said he would rather look at water than at me."[16]

In terms of plot, not much action occurs in "The Water Faucet Vision." Callie narrates the fighting between her parents that escalates to Helen's fall and emergency room visit, and she narrates Patty's grief over her father's abandonment and his subsequent return a month later. She also tells readers about the miracles that she had hoped to perform as a martyr, describing herself as "the kind of girl who grows morbid in Catholic school, who longs to be chopped or frozen to death but then has nightmares about it from which she wakes up screaming and clutching a stuffed bear"; yet as Callie goes on to explain, what truly soothed her was not a stuffed toy but "a string of three malachite beads," which she squeezed anytime she found herself in an anxious place.[17] The loss of these beads following the domestic violence between her parents left Callie bereft, producing an "agony all out of proportion to my string of pretty beads," as Callie says; "I hadn't cried at all during my mother's accident, but now I was crying all afternoon, all through dinner, and then after dinner, too—crying past the point where I knew what I was crying for."[18] As readers can surmise, Callie projected the grief and instability she felt over her parents' fighting and Ralph's violence against Helen onto her missing beads. The adult narrator chooses this moment in the past to connect with her mother's death in the present to signal that the childhood fear and anxiety that Callie had about her mother dying have now actually come to pass.

The story ends in a vision that Callie has of lights flashing, the smell of coffee, and the experience of the room turning cold, and then "a perfectly middle-aged man's voice, speaking something very like pig Latin, told me not to despair, my beads would be returned to me."[19] Callie's interpretation of this vision results in her turning on all the faucets in their home, believing that the beads would return to her through the town's water system. Of course when her family awakens to the house being flooded, the honest Callie fesses up, leading Mona to tell everyone about her sister's visions at their Catholic school, which Callie says marked the end to her "saintly ambitions."[20] However, the story ends with Callie wistfully thinking back on her Catholic school days: "Back then, the world was a place that could be set right. One had only to direct the hand of the Almighty and say, Just here, Lord, we hurt here—and here, and here, and here."[21] Callie's adult pain over the loss of her mother will not be soothed by the return of a strand of malachite beads or the succor of her former faith; yet as the final line indicates, it is comforting and compelling to believe in a lost world that could be righted through devotion.

The story that precedes "The Water Faucet Vision," "Birthmates" (1994), was originally published in *Ploughshares* and received the distinction of being selected for the 1995 *Best American Short Stories* by the guest editor Jane Smiley and for *The Best American Short Stories of the Century*, edited by John Updike. This last honor is made all the more distinct since Jen's work is the only one included that was written by an Asian American author with a Chinese American protagonist. The main action occurs in December in an unnamed urban city beset by snow, where Art goes to attend an industry trade show on minicomputers, which the heterodiegetic narrator calls "a dinosaur industry."[22] To save money, Art finds the cheapest lodging in the area, which turns out to be a welfare hotel. Fearing that an intruder will break in since his window leads out onto a fire escape, Art removes the telephone handset from its console to use as a potential weapon; it was "an old handset, the hefty kind that made you feel the seriousness of human communication."[23] This handset will prove to be the source of Art's misfortune, although it is more accurate to say that Art's decision to remove the handset to use as a weapon is the real problem—and perhaps even further, that his insistence on staying at the cheapest hotel he could find rather than in the cheapest room in the conference hotel is indicative of his antihero status: he is a man who acts, but his decisions lead to unfortunate consequences.

One of those unfortunate consequences is his divorce from his wife Lisa. Although neither Lisa nor Art is ever named by ethnicity or race, the omniscient narrator provides indirect clues, such as Art's surname, Woo, and the detail that "Lisa had grown up on the West Coast. She was full of Asian conscious-ness."[24] Another clue is that Art is taunted by children in the lobby the morning after he arrives at the hotel, with one child reciting, "Ching chong polly wolly wing wong"[25] at Art, the mocking verse used against Asians in America to sig-nal their racialized difference.[26] Art has walked into the lobby full of children and mothers where "almost everyone was black; the white children stood out like little missed opportunities."[27] Art's recognition of his racial difference from those of the children, as well as the racial difference of the white children from the black kids, ones that the simile of "missed opportunities" refers to, signals that Art and/or the narrator believe that the white children, like Art, are somehow not supposed to be at the welfare hotel.

Art has his racial ideas challenged when he is knocked down and eventu-ally knocked out by the elementary-school-aged children in the lobby, who use the telephone handset against Art—the same telephone handset that Art takes from his hotel room down to the lobby since he believes that he needs such a weapon to protect himself from the dangerous elements in this neighborhood. When he comes to, he is in the room of an African American former nurse, Cindy, who provides hot milk and honey and two Tylenol tablets from Art's briefcase. When Cindy tells Art, "This ain't no place for a nice boy like you," Art replies that it is not a place fit for Cindy and her children either, to which she says, "That's how the Almighty planned it, right? You folk rise up while we set and watch."[28]

The phrase "you folk" continues to nag at Art throughout the day, as he sets up his booth at the trade show. He does indulge in some light erotic fantasies about knocking on Cindy's door and after coitus rescuing her and her children "from their dead-end life," since "he couldn't sleep with a woman like Cindy and then leave her flat. She could *you folk* him, he could never *us folk* her."[29] Even in his imagination Art realizes the reality of class and race that separates him from Cindy. While Art Woo as Chinese American may not be a significant factor in his interactions with his fellow residents of the welfare hotel, Art Woo as Asian American and as a middle-class businessman who is a temporary guest and can leave of his own volition is differentiated from the children and moth-ers in the lobby, and Art Woo as a minority seen to be a model citizen, one of the ones who is seemingly rising above black and brown fellow minorities, is part of the "you folk" that Cindy claims him to be, which she says "with so little rancor, with something so like intimacy."[30] This is the power of Jen's craft as a writer. This story is and is not about race and racial differences because this story is about the failures of Art—his failures in his professional life, which lead him to be staying at a welfare hotel instead of the conference site; his failures as a father, since he and Lisa were unable to have children, the last attempt resulting in the termination of the pregnancy when they discovered that their unborn child had brittle bone disease; and the failure of his marriage to Lisa, a marriage that could not be maintained amid her grief over three failed pregnancies. Yet Art also fails to understand the dynamics of race and class that govern his relationship with Cindy and the other welfare hotel residents. He is stuck thinking about Cindy's phrase "you folk," recognizing that he cannot claim unity with Cindy but also desiring a connection with her because he desires connection and intimacy with anyone; another one of his many failures is his inability to sustain such human familiarity.

The story ends tragicomically. Art is aided by a fellow trade show attendee, Ernie, who sends a head hunter to him. The head hunter, whom the narrator describes as looking like St. Francis of Assisi, tells Art that he knows someone who may be interested in hiring him and that that person will ring him at his hotel to set up a breakfast meeting. Elated, Art imagines a new life for himself: "He was moving on, moving west. There would be a good job there, and a new life. Perhaps he would take up tennis. Perhaps he would own a Jacuzzi. Perhaps he would learn to like all those peculiar foods people ate out there, like jicama and seaweed."[31] However Art's daydreams about restarting his life out west come to an abrupt end when he realizes that the handset to his phone is still missing since he failed to retrieve it from the kids who attacked him that morning. In the final scene of this story Art is alone in his room watching someone climb up the fire escape, which is the scenario that caused him to unplug the receiver from the phone in the first place. When the shadow does not stop at Art's window, he recalls again Cindy's phrase "you folk" and acknowledges that he "could see her perspective; he was luckier than she, by far."[32] Yet the last image that the narrator leaves readers with is of Art Woo feeling as if he is drowning—his distance from his former wife and any hopeful future of a happy home life seemingly as remote as the disappeared phone handset and their baby son. The last line hauntingly shows the consequences and costs of Art's many failures, as he reflects on the ultrasound of his unborn son: "Transparent, he had looked, and gelatinous, all soft head and quick heart; but he would have, in being born, broken every bone in his body."[33]

Following "Birthmates," Jen's next short fiction works were published in 1998: "Lulu in Exile" (*New York Times* magazine), "Chin" (*Shorts*, Granta Books), "Just Wait" (*Ploughshares*), and "Who's Irish?" (*New Yorker*). All but "Lulu in Exile" are included in *Who's Irish? Stories*, although traces of "Lulu in Exile" appear in "Duncan in China." "Just Wait," like most of Jen's other short fiction works, particularly those employing heterodiegetic narration, is not temporally marked by historic events or other elements that situate it in a specific time period other than the present moment. Furthermore this story, like most of Jen's fiction both short and long, appears set in the Northeast, in this case an unnamed city that is probably Boston since the protagonist Addie Wing grew up in a suburb outside of Boston, has a piece of art hanging in the Museum of Fine Arts,[34] and has a husband who "did low income housing in the inner city."[35] The heterodiegetic narration focuses on the pregnant Addie Wing and opens with her baby shower and the gift of a camcorder bestowed on her by her three brothers: the middle child, who goes by Will and has done so for the last twenty years but whom both Addie and the omniscient narrator refer to as Billy; Mark Lee, the youngest and a stepbrother, his father, Reynolds, ostensibly having marred their mother, Regina, after Addie's father died and while she was too young to have memories of him; and the oldest brother, Neddie, who has signed the card but is absent from the gathering because he has been hospitalized for mental illness. The story's title seems to refer, most directly, to the soon-to-be-born baby of Addie and her husband, Rex. As with "Birthmates" and nearly all of Jen's other short fiction, the racial and ethnic identities of the characters are not clearly stated but can be inferred and interpreted through surnames and oblique textual references. While Billy is described by Mark as being "a nice Chinese boy," Mark is seemingly racially unmarked except for his last name, Lee.[36] Given Jen's previous track record in writing about Chinese Americans, one can safely assume that Mark is also Chinese American. As for Addie's husband, we do not learn his surname, but we do discover that his mother, Doreen, is "a Nisei from Hawaii," which would then make Rex a Sansei or third-generation Japanese American.[37] While there will be readers who are unfamiliar with the term "Nisei" and therefore will not understand that this is an ethnic code word, the narrator tells us a few pages later that Rex's "mother's father had been a Buddhist priest in Japan," thus alerting readers to Rex's ethnic difference and racial similarity to Addie's family.

However, "Just Wait" does not concentrate on issues of race or ethnicity. The Chineseness or Japaneseness of these characters' ancestries is almost entirely incidental to the action, behaviors, and thoughts of these characters. The story is most centrally focused on the theme of family—the intimacies and ruptures and tensions that occur within families. The first half of the story takes place at the baby shower, with the narrator's focalization contained to Addie's perspective. Postshower the omniscient narrator does provide insight into Rex's musings on Addie's pregnancy and the changes he sees in her, but the remainder of "Just Wait" returns to Addie's focalization and her preoccupations with family, particularly what to do about her mother, Regina, who is also referred to as Madame Lee. Both names are appropriate for Addie's imperious mother, who does not believe in helping out during parties because it makes her feel like a servant and who is horrified at the prospect of having to assist with her soon-to-be grandchild. This last point is raised by the shower guests when Regina dramatically reveals, through an inappropriate regifting of a stuffed sailfish, that she and Reynolds are getting a divorce, leaving her without a home.

Addie thus finds herself, postshower, turning her office into Regina's room and, with the help of her brothers, converting a kitchen closet into her new work space. Both Addie and Rex are described as do-gooder types whose incomes are commensurate with the activist and artistic registers of their work and whose work finds either disapproval or disparagement from their parents. Doreen had hoped that Rex would be a doctor rather than someone dedicated to improving low-income housing projects, and Addie became a garden designer "who took small spaces and simply made them beautiful," giving up a career as an artist just as she was gaining some renown: "She had, in fact, just had a piece of hers hung at the Museum of Fine Arts right opposite a Lucien Freud when she realized that art was over for her."[38] In many ways this story is about the smallness of domestic life—about the prosaic nature of waiting for a baby during pregnancy, of waiting to see if parents will stop being disappointed about the life choices of their children, of waiting to see if people can stay in their do-gooder careers or, as Rex wonders, "whether he couldn't trade in, say, half of his unimpeachable integrity for cash."[39]

The anticipation hinted at in the title finds fruition in the story's last paragraph as Addie, looking over the blueprints for her new office, begins to go into labor. Her waiting for her child will soon be over, "her mind turning, fearfully, toward labor."[40] Yet the last image that Jen leaves us with is not Addie's anxiety over the birth of her child but her wistfulness over missing her brother Neddie and her hope that one day he will be able to meet her child. Imagining the scene of Neddie greeting his future niece or nephew, Addie pictures him opening up his arms and commenting on this newest edition, *How nice to have a new stranger in the family.*[41] "Just Wait" illustrates the ways in which family members can feel strange and disconnected and yet, at the same time, how this bond of kinship, whether through blood or marriage, sustains and uplifts.

"Chin," the sixth piece in the collection and the shortest at nine pages, follows "Just Wait" and shares with that story an ambiguity of when but not where, as we are told by the unnamed homodiegetic adolescent male narrator that the story takes place on Central Avenue "in scenic Yonkers, New York."[42] The scenic reference is made ironically; the narrator's family lives in a first-floor apartment, euphemistically called a "garden apartment," as does the subject of this story, a boy whom the narrator calls simply Chin. Jen's short fiction is often short on plot, with much of the action of her narratives occurring through the internal musings of the various protagonists and rendered either through omniscient or first-person narration. In this way "Chin" is like many of Jen's other short stories, and yet it departs from the other pieces in the collection and in Jen's short fiction oeuvre in the race of its narrator-protagonist, who, though of unspecified race, is most certainly not Chinese American since his family "came from Yonkers and didn't have no special foods, unless you wanted to count fries," and when people asked him what his family was, he replied, "Vanilla."[43] Like its literary predecessors *Moby-Dick* and *The Great Gatsby*, this story focuses on someone other than the first-person narrator, in this case the titular Chin, who is a Chinese American classmate of the narrator and whose family lives in an adjacent building to that of the narrator's family, so that the goings-on of the Chin family can be seen and heard by the narrator's family as if they are watching a television program. As the narrator explains, "We could see everything and hear everything they did over there, especially if we turned the TV down, which we sometimes did for a fight. If only more was in English, we could've understood everything too."[44] Beyond the fighting, the narrator observes, "Nights he wasn't getting beaten up, he was parked in front of the blackboard doing equations with his pa," which are some of the only times the narrator recounts the father and son interacting free of violence.[45]

Fighting is the theme in young Chin's life, as the story opens with his narrator-neighbor announcing, "I wasn't his friend, but I wasn't one of the main kids who hounded him up on the shed of the roof."[46] Chin's life, as focalized through the adolescent narrator, is fraught with bruises, as he must fend off the rocks thrown at him by the neighborhood bullies who torment him and he must endure the beatings at home by his taxi-driving father, a man who had been a doctor back in China and now finds himself with a mouth infection that creates so many bills that his wife is forced to work at a dry cleaner's. In this brief story the narrator's family spends much of their time wondering about their neighbors and making guesses about their lives, often based on stereotypes. For example the narrator's mother believes that their neighbors never open the windows of their apartment because people from China "liked their apartment hot, seeing as how it was what they were used to,"[47] and the narrator's friend Gus tells him that the reason Chin can climb up a roof so quickly to escape his tormentors is "on account of there was monkey feet inside his sneakers."[48] Indeed what seems clear from the narrator's conjectures is that neither he nor his family has any real experience with people of Chinese ancestry, even though, as his mother notes, "they were getting to be a fact of life. Not like in California or Queens, but they were definitely proliferating, along with a lot of other people who could tell you where they came from, if they spoke English."[49]

Although the time period is ambiguous in this story, references to "getting a JD card" and being beat on the hand with a ruler signal that this is an era where corporal punishment is an accepted practice in schools and juvenile delinquency is something to be feared.[50] However, the narrator's comment about the irony relating to Chin's excelling in history and English but not in math and science suggests that perhaps this story is taking place in the 1980s, a time when the model minority myth of Asian excellence in STEM (Science, Technology, Engineering, and Mathematics) fields predominated but when actual Asian Americans had not yet moved into suburban New York spaces. In many ways the specificity of time period is not important because it is the acute sense of Chin's alienation seen through the narrator's eyes that forms the crux of this story. Violence and abuse are part of Chin's daily life, so much so that when the voyeuristic narrator watches Chin's father beat him on his naked back with a garden stake, the narrator confesses, "Sometimes I think I should've kept my eyes on the TV where they belonged, instead of watching stuff I couldn't turn off."[51]

However, the narrator, like the rest of his family, continues to watch the fighting of the neighbors, which culminates in the last scene of the story. After Chin's sister tries to intervene during one particular beating, telling her father that she will move out of the house because of his abuse, she too is beaten. Their mother packs a suitcase and leaves the house with the sister but not Chin. The mother and daughter walk toward the bus stop in the snow, stopping to "[have] themselves a little conference. . . . They jawed for a long time. Then they moved a little farther up the incline and stopped and jawed again."[52] As evident from the language used by the narrator here and elsewhere in the story, his is a working-class family employing a working-class diction, his class status affirmed by his fireman father and his sister's hairdresser fiancé. His father, a man who rescues people professionally, wants to help his female neighbors but is not sure how to provide assistance as he sits "in the window with the lights on, waiting for the Chin women to shout Fire! or something, I guess. He wanted them to behold him there, all lit up, their rescuer."[53] While his father watches the Chin women, the narrator keeps an eye on the male family members, only to find "the most astounding thing of all: they were back at the blackboard, working problems out. Mr. Chin had a cup of tea made, and you couldn't see his face on account of his bandage, but he was gesturing with the eraser and Chin was nodding. How do you figure?"[54] The answer, of course, is that neither the narrator nor his Yonkers family will ever understand the dynamics of their immigrant Chinese American neighbors. The narrator's father will not come to the rescue of the Chin women, for the last line of the story tells readers that "they dragged their broken suitcase straight back across our view," signaling their return home.[55] While it is unclear how sympathetic the narrator is toward his Chinese American neighbors, readers are clearly meant to empathize with the plight of the Chin family, who are struggling with money, with bullying, and with how far they are from being part of the American dream.

In contrast to the struggling Chinese immigrant family in "Chin," Jen's title story, "Who's Irish?," the one that begins the collection, features a Chinese American family that has seemingly achieved the American dream. The homodiegetic narrator, like the narrator in "Chin," is unnamed, but we learn that she is a sixty-eight-year-old Chinese immigrant widow and retired restaurant owner who lives with her daughter Natalie, her son-in-law John Shea, and their three-year-old daughter, Sophie, in a house that is large enough that they all have their own rooms. Although her daughter has been newly named vice president of a bank, there is "no money left over, because only one income, but lucky enough, got the baby-sitter for free."[56] Despite John's being unemployed at the beginning of the story, the narrator tells us, "So my son-in-law can be man, I am baby-sitter" because even though "he has no job," he "cannot take care of Sophie either. Because he is a man, he say, and that's the end of the sentence."[57] As these quotes make clear, the narrator speaks in a pidgin English to signal her Chinese immigrant status, which is also announced in the story through her not so politically correct musings about John's family. Not understanding why the four Shea brothers are all unemployed, the narrator rhetorically wonders, "Why the Shea family have so much trouble? They are white people, they speak English."[58] Comparing the Chinese with the Irish, the narrator not so subtly implies that the Sheas' unemployment is due to their ethnicity. First she says, "I always thought the Irish people are like Chinese people, work so hard on the railroad, but now I know why the Chinese beat the Irish,"[59] and next she compares her situation to the Irish American Sheas: "When I come to this country, I have no money and do not speak English. But my husband and I own our restaurant before he die. Free and clear, no mortgage. Of course, I understand I am lucky, come from a country where the food is popular all over the world. I understand it is not the Shea family's fault they come from a country where everything is boiled."[60] Exhibiting her trademark wit, Jen skewers both Irish and Chinese American stereotypes through the voice of this Chinese immigrant mother, who records with eagle eyes the cultural differences among the Chinese, the Irish, and their Americanized children and mixed-race grandchildren.

The central conflict in "Who's Irish?" is indeed one of culture, as the unnamed narrator finds her granddaughter to have "her nice Chinese side swallowed up by her wild Shea side."[61] Sophie's previous babysitter Amy had encouraged Sophie to do as she pleased, and Sophie's parents forbid the narrator to spank her granddaughter when she misbehaves. Although the narrator tries to follow her daughter's advice, when Sophie continues to act out, the narrator spanks her, resulting in Sophie's compliance and the narrator's hiding from her daughter her new means of behavioral control. Although Sophie behaves herself for a while, soon the permissiveness of American culture intrudes, as she learns that she can kick adults from her four-year-old friend, Sinbad, who throws sand at his mother from a foxhole he digs in the playground and kicks her. Sinbad tells Sophie to kick his mother: "Sophie kick her. A little kick."[62] The narrator punishes Sophie, spanking her and insisting that she apologize to Sinbad's mother, but the mother tells Sophie that it is OK. "After that, Sophie learn she can attack mommies in the playground, and some will say Stop, but others will say, Oh, she didn't mean it, especially if they realize Sophie will be punished."[63] The American mothers' reliance on the immigrant grandmother to enact punishment while they remain passive in the face of Sophie's inappropriate behavior speaks to the cultural differences that the narrator sees between Chinese and American society; Sophie may be misbehaving, but in U.S. culture it is up to the parents and guardians, not community members or strangers, to keep children in check. What the narrator observes from Sophie's interaction with the mothers whom she kicks is that they will implicitly sanction her behavior by saying it is OK to be kicked so long as they know that punishment will come in the form of the grandmother's spanking of Sophie.

Throughout this story the narrator comments on the differences between her Chinese daughter Natalie and her wild granddaughter Sophie. She believes that Sophie's wildness is a result of her Irish heritage, repeating the refrain that Chinese children do not act the way that Sophie acts. The tensions between the narrator and Sophie and the narrator and Natalie erupt after one particularly bad playground experience between Sophie and her grandmother. When Sophie ambushes the narrator with a shovelful of sand in just the same way that Sinbad had attacked his mother, the narrator admonishes Sophie and insists that she come out of the foxhole and apologize to her. But Sophie, knowing that there are consequences to her actions from her "Meanine" grandmother, remains in the foxhole, even after the narrator says that she "yell, yell, yell, and what happen? Nothing. A Chinese mother would help, but American mothers, they look at you, they shake their head, they go home. And, of course, a Chinese child would give up, but not Sophie."[64] When it becomes dark, the grandmother "try to use a stick, chase her out of there, and once or twice I hit her, but still she does not come out."[65] When Natalie and John come to the playground, John crawls into the foxhole to retrieve his daughter and discovers "bruises all over her brown skin, and a swollen-up eye," which are the consequences of the narrator's Chinese parenting style, one that is violent and harmful to her granddaughter.[66]

Repeating the phrase "I took care of her," the narrator recounts how she parented her daughter when she was a baby, telling readers, "A daughter I have, a beautiful daughter. I took care of her when she could not hold her head up. I took care of her before she could argue with me, when she was a little girl with two pigtails, one of them always crooked. I took care of her when we have to escape from China, I took care of her when suddenly we live in a country with cars everywhere, if you are not careful your little girl get run over."[67] In this refrain is a lament over the child whom the narrator once loved, cherished, and protected during a time when Natalie was young and vulnerable—a time before her Americanized daughter would find herself in conflict with her Chinese immigrant mother. After the playground incident, the daughter tells her mother that she can no longer live with them: "She say she have no choice, she doesn't want to end up divorced."[68] But before the narrator is moved into a solo apartment, John's mother, Bess, a retired executive secretary and fellow widow, extends an invitation to the narrator to move in with her. Earlier in the story Bess is described as good-natured and not so politically correct, as she tells the narrator, "I was never against the marriage, you know . . . I never thought John was marrying down. I always thought Nattie was just as good as white."[69] In this statement Bess's bigotry comes through, just as the prejudices of the narrator are similarly pronounced.

Yet by ending with the two widowed women together, keeping each other company, Jen suggests that these prejudices can be put aside or forgotten through other means of solidarity, such as the comfort of having someone of a similar age and place in life to watch television with—"to have some female company."[70] The ending of the story also shows that despite one's advanced age, people can change their formerly narrow minds, as Bess seems to do through her invitation to the narrator to make herself at home in her home and through her admonishment to her sons, who pointedly ask the narrator when she is going home, "but Bess tell them, Get lost. She's a permanent resident, say Bess. She isn't going anywhere."[71] As the literary critic Rachel Lee noted in a book review of *Who's Irish? Stories,* the invocation of the phrase "permanent resident" "evokes an idiom of the Immigration and Naturalization service,"[72] conjuring up a not so distant past in which Asians were the targets of racist laws restricting them from becoming either citizens or permanent residents.[73] The final paragraph of the story introduces the title of the story. The narrator laughs at Bess's suggestion that she become an honorary Irish and exclaims, "Me! Who's Irish?"[74] Although both Bess and the narrator laugh at this seemingly preposterous suggestion, Bess's words *Permanent Resident. Not going anywhere*" repeat in the narrator's head, as she tells us, "Over and over I hear it, the voice of Bess."[75] As already demonstrated in Jen's second novel, it is possible for people to switch and to find new homes where they least expect them.

While *Who's Irish?* is mostly comprised of Jen's previously published short fiction, there are two original pieces in this collection, "Duncan in China" and "House, House, Home," that feature Chinese American protagonists. In consistently writing about nonwhite, specifically Chinese American, characters Jen draws attention to issues of ethnicity and race, even if the focus and themes of the story are not especially racially or ethnically oriented. In other words, by having a contemporary American writer, such as Jen, write about American characters who are Asian and Chinese American in universal situations, Jen expands our ideas about the kinds of work that should be included in the American literary canon and the kinds of characters we see as American.

"Duncan in China," the fourth story in the collection, has roots in a short story that Jen published in the *New York Times* magazine, "Lulu in Exile" (1998). In this earlier piece Jen explores the family dynamics of two brothers, Arnie and Jefferson, the former a successful businessman with a beautiful Hong Kong girlfriend, Lulu, and the latter a failure who constantly disappoints his mother. In "Duncan in China," Jen has kept the concept of having two brothers, one successful and one a failure, but has changed the name of the failed brother to Duncan and turns the focus to him rather than to the Hong Kong girlfriend. In many ways this is the most American of Jen's stories, because its hero, Duncan Hsu, is most acutely aware of being an American amid the people of his mother's motherland. The heterodiegetic narrator opens the narrative with "Duncan Hsu, foreign expert. That was his name in China."[76] Many Asians in America are treated by mainstream society as if they are foreigners, even those who are born here and who, like Duncan, have never set foot in their ancestral homelands. By setting the story in China and placing an American of Chinese descent in the center of the inevitable cultural clashes, Jen provides a subtle critique to the idea of Asian Americans as foreign by literally making her American character a "foreign expert" in China—a stranger in a strange land, even if he superficially and phenotypically resembles the people in his host country.

Duncan, a dropout from military school, law school, and a computer-programming class, is in China to teach English language to students in a coal-mining institute, which is an autobiographical detail from Jen's own life since, like her fictional creation, she taught English at the Shandong Mining College after being deemed a failure by her parents for dropping out of an M.B.A. program. The story explores the many differences that the American foreigner encounters with life in communist China: the lack of basic amenities, such as heat; the lack of culinary variety, because of the necessity to eat what is in season rather than what can be obtained through supermarket chains; and the need always to be chaperoned and to have excursions approved by party leaders, as Duncan has requested to visit with distant relatives who live up north. Yet despite these cultural and national differences, in many ways this story explores the universal theme of how to handle difficult coworkers. In Duncan's case, the teacher assigned to guide him through his time in China, Professor Mo, is a rather unctuous and officious man who seeks his own comfort above others and who uses his role as Duncan's guide as a pretext to enjoy the scant luxuries that Duncan has been provided, such as extra heat in the winter and trips to Beijing and the scenic mountain Tai Shan. Duncan initially tries to navigate his relationship with Mo cautiously, but eventually he asserts his own preferences and desires over Mo's edicts, actions that will have consequences for him when Mo writes a report against Duncan for inappropriate behavior with a female student.

This female student, Louise (all the English-language students give themselves English names in the story), is an object of Duncan's affections, but due to the scrutiny of the Chinese government as well as the school officials, the most intimate act between them occurs when they sit on top of Tai Shan mountain just after sunrise. The belief among the *lao taitai*—old women who make a pilgrimage to the mountaintop—is that at dawn, when the sun appears to leap into the sky, "they might look into their hearts, purifying themselves. Then they could make a request of Buddha."[77] The conversation between Louise and Duncan on the mountaintop is the most personal of their acquaintance, as Louise asks Duncan about his request and Duncan says, "I asked the Buddha that I might find love."[78] Although Duncan had not done this, the omniscient narrator tells us that "he realized, now, accepted now, that he was speaking in a kind of translation," hoping that Louise will understand his meaning and perhaps reciprocate his feelings, as he has fantasized about taking her back with him to the United States when his contract expires.[79] Louise, however, has other plans and demurs from Duncan's veiled allusions to romance, even as she tells him that her own request to the Buddha is for Duncan to be introduced to someone special.

Although Duncan is disappointed, he has experienced, just prior to their conversation, a type of epiphany on the mountaintop. Watching the sunrise along with the *lao taitai,* Duncan "felt a twinge of envy for the *lao taitai,* who did not seem desperate at all, but full of peace, full of an old, large faith that would never live for him. It was he who was desperate—godless, modern man."[80] Closing his eyes, however, leads Duncan to realize that "he had much in his heart. For what was he but a free man who had rejected much and embraced little? He was a free man who had never truly loved. He was a free man who believed nothing in particular, who did nothing in particular. He was a free man who had not even embraced his freedom."[81] The repetition of Duncan being "a free man" contrasts with the constraints of his Chinese colleagues and students. It is also a contrast between the values of the traditional and distinctly unmodern China versus those of the forward-thinking and permissive modern Western society.[82] However, as the omniscient narrator illustrates, Duncan has taken this freedom for granted and made little of it since he has neither faith nor love in his life—he does not even have an ideology he believes in since he does not even embrace the freedom that he now recognizes as his birthright, as the birthright of all Americans.

After this excursion Louise is sent away from the college charged with immoral behavior based on a classmate's, William's, report (he was also on the Tai Shan excursion) and written up by Duncan's colleague and nemesis, Professor Mo. Duncan, again accompanied by Mo, meets up with his cousin Guotai and Guotai's son, Bing Bing, in Beijing. Feeling depressed and guilty about his privilege and prosperity as a foreign expert, Duncan entertains the thought of adopting Bing Bing, especially after hearing Guotai's stories of surviving the Cultural Revolution, which left him a broken man struggling to feed his seven-year-old son and his wife, who has been diagnosed with tuberculosis. However, when he returns back to his room in the mining college, he finds that Louise has returned, accompanied by her nineteen-year-old daughter, Lingli, who is apparently the someone special she had alluded to on top of Tai Shan.

The story ends with the internal musings of Duncan, who imagines different possibilities for Louise's actions, for his possible reactions, and for his feelings toward her and her daughter and wonders whether he should take Lingli with him when he returns to the United States or whether "it was possible he could never forgive himself if he sponsored Lingli to the United States and left poor Guotai and Bing Bing behind."[83] This last paragraph focuses on the different possibilities that Duncan may encounter, which returns to the theme of freedom gleaned from his epiphany on Tai Shan. Unlike his brother Arnie (who fixates on making money) or the *lao taitai* (whose Buddhist faith keeps them climbing a mountaintop in their advanced age), Duncan has no purpose in life; he has no cause with which to devote himself. Yet what he has is his national birthright: "There was the one thing he had, being an American—not so much an unshakable conviction as a habit of believing in the happiest possibility. Truly it was a form of blindness. He understood why denizens of the Old World laughed at people like him. Yet he saw now, finally, that it was incurably his as any faith."[84] Duncan's faith is that he can have faith: blind, hopeful faith. He has the privilege of being an American who can dream big, who can hope and see possibilities with happy outcomes, despite practical obstacles and difficulties. The story ends, appropriately, with Duncan imagining his life as a movie, with Lingli possibly starring as his leading lady: "How vividly he could imagine the scenes and the credits; and, after the credits, the applause."[85] It is Duncan's American faith and the hope that accompanies his national culture that allow him to imagine his life in such cinematic turns with such widespread approval. Only in America can an American dropout dream such big dreams about his return home.

The last story in *Who's Irish?* is the longest of Jen's published short fiction and could be considered a novella in terms of its length and scope, which covers over a decade of its protagonist's life. "House, House, Home" begins and ends in the present time period of Pammie Lee, who, as we learn from the heterodiegetic narrator, is at her elementary-school-aged daughter's school to help out with "the children of color lunch."[86] Jen uses this event as a way to depict comically the ways that children interpret and internalize racial and ethnic issues and identities. Pammie wonders "if any of the kids knew what a child of color was, and whether they were supposed to have figured this out for themselves,"[87] as Pammie's job is to find students who self-select as children of color to attend a lunch that she recognizes "was too much about adult paradigms."[88] As white children announce themselves to be pink, with one declaring that she will attend because her au pair is from Montana and with black children declining and Asian American kids ambivalent about attending, Jen shows the truly socially constructed nature of connecting race with color and children's interpretations of their own identities when it comes to a term such as "children of color."

Besides skewering racial dynamics, we also learn some basic information about the protagonist Pammie from these opening pages: she is in her mid-thirties; she has three children; she has an ex-husband, Sven; and she has volunteered to be on the school's diversity committee, which is how she ends up meeting her future Hawaiian lover-boyfriend-partner Carter. In "House, House, Home," Jen experiments with a new way of signaling dialogue among her characters through a tabbed em dash and no quotation marks so that speech and exposition run together, a combination of direct quotes and indirect discourse mingled together, as the initial meeting between Carter and Pammie demonstrates:

—A fellow yellow person, he said. His gaze likewise seemed unusually pointed, and fixed.
—Yes, she said, as though it were still a major event to be met with a fellow Asian in this town.[89]

As can be discerned from this dialogue as well as the opening pages of the story, it is the late 1990s, one of the few times Jen gives us specific temporal markers to fix the narrative, and Pammie and Carter live in the Northeast, where Asian Americans are still a distinct minority, despite Pammie's claim that it is no longer a major event to encounter a fellow yellow person in their town.

"House, House, Home" tells the story of how Pammie ended up divorced with three children and potentially newly partnered with a man so different from her first husband, which essentially is the story of how she grew from young adulthood into full adulthood. In an extended analepsis, the omniscient narrator flashes back to Pammie's days in college when she first meets Sven, who at fifty-two is old enough to be her father and who is, in fact, her art history professor. After their relationship becomes public, which begins while Pammie is still enrolled in his course, Sven is summarily fired (perhaps aided by the fact that he was an ABD lecturer and not a tenured professor). In an effort to make their illicit affair more legitimate, they get married at city hall, which the narrator characterizes as "an aesthetic decision. For was this not called for? That they should be carried away, that the drama should broaden and lead on?"[90]

What we, the readers, learn over the course of their ten-year marriage are the ways that Pammie and Sven eventually grow apart or, perhaps more accurately, the ways that Pammie matures beyond Sven, who grows more rigid rather than relaxed as she had hoped: "She realized later that she had assumed his age would stabilize their relationship, that his increasing vulnerability would make him more likely to accept imperfections in his living arrangements."[91] Among the imperfections that Sven finds hardest to cope with are his children, whom he loves but whom he parents haphazardly and reluctantly. In the initial bloom of their newlywed state, and as a bulwark to the judgments of society and Pammie's family, she and Sven announce themselves to be against all that is bourgeois, immersing themselves with a bohemian group of friends, buying a loft, and living off Sven's half-million dollars: "They lived at the beginning in a kind of delirium of freedom from such concerns, and from the past and their families as well."[92] "Such concerns" include matters of money, and one of the sources of tension that appear in their marriage is over their different class statuses, since Pammie surmises from the things Sven does and does not share that he had once upon a time accumulated much more than the half-million in his bank account, allowing him to be a man who could dedicate himself to studying art without the necessity of a paycheck.

Pammie's inferior class status (as perceived by Sven) is another of the imperfections of their living arrangement, because Pammie, as one of eight children raised by Chinese immigrant parents, has a very different relationship with her relations than Sven does with his; his parents are deceased, and he has no relatives with whom he keeps in touch. Pammie's close-knit Chinese American family grates on Sven, and they in turn register their disregard for him by introducing him to friends at family events as "my son-in-law, who doesn't eat Chinese food."[93] An inverse of Ralph Chang's boasting about his son-in-law Seth Mandel in *Mona in the Promised Land,* the declaration that Sven does not eat Chinese food demonstrates his lack of affinity with not only Chinese culture but also with the values of the Lee family. Sven's age, his class snobbery, and his cultural differences from the Lees create a wedge between Pammie and her family, even though they never formally disown her. While initially Pammie seems untroubled by this rift, realizing that "she, for her part, had married him, to facilitate her leave-taking" from her family, after the birth of her first child, Adam, she desires a connection with them so that Adam might have company through his many cousins.[94]

Sven, however, dismisses Pammie's desire to increase their family beyond their own small sphere, and after the birth two years later of their daughter Sophie, he finds his wife to be suffering from the same middle-class and middle-brow ailment as does her family: "The opposite of marvelous had always been bourgeois. That was the label they had used for Pammie's family, for example. Sven used to call them people whose ambitions could be satisfied in department stores. But now Pammie was bourgeois too, and so were all of her ideas about child rearing, particularly the ones that involved making sure the children were part of their community."[95] Sven has no use for community, whether of family, of work, or of friends. He also has no use for a partner who has opinions and a life and a career that are not of his influence. He accuses Pammie of rebelling against him when she switches her interest from visual art to architecture. Sven, on the other hand, is described by the narrator as the kind of man "who firmly believed that wonderful monographs could be written by nonexperts," a conclusion he makes after deciding to pursue the study of Asian art, a field he is not trained in but one "he had grown interested in . . . since their marriage."[96] Sven's objectification of his wife also happens along gendered lines, as he tells her, "A woman has only to think of others to be a woman. . . . A man without work is not a man."[97]

In skewering Sven, Jen also skewers the myopia of white male privilege. In the waning days of their marriage, Pammie and Sven find themselves arguing about "who was more genuinely an outsider, he who had had the vision and will to refuse an acceptance that was his birthright, or she who had been born on the margin and only quite slowly earned a conditional pass."[98] In a clear articulation of the key racial difference between Sven and their children, Pammie tells him, "Your confidence was conferred on you by society. Your children do not look like you and will be granted no such thing. We need to think what the sources of their power will be, that they will not be constantly kicked by little people trying to make themselves feel better."[99] Pammie comes to realize that

Sven is one of the little people who treats others as inferior in order to make himself feel better: "It was the talk of the nineties, of a new generation—how she had been wifed, how she had been fetishized, how she had been viewed as Orientallia."[100] The brilliance of this story is that Jen does not depict Pammie as an agentless victim and does not make "House, House, Home" a warning tale against young college women marrying their older, white male art history professors. The story is without a moral; it is instead a chronicle of Pammie's independence—from Sven but also from Carter's own intellectual and activist beliefs, which Pammie sometimes experiences as a tidal wave but one she can withstand since "it was only a matter of inhabiting, with a certain adamance, herself."[101]

Herself is what Pammie learns to embrace. The last paragraph of the story has Pammie declaring herself to be an adult and offers a rumination on an architectural term, "*poches*—the nondescript pockets left, for example, by a circular room inscribed in a square. Enigmatic spaces, they were."[102] Enigmatic spaces are an apt metaphor for Jen's short fiction, particularly the ones collected in *Who's Irish? Stories*. Her tales are in between spaces—pockets that are on the margins of more discernible and mainstream social spheres. Pammie's appreciation for poches leads her to declare "how they enlivened the spaces they made possible," a wonderful description of the cumulative effect of reading each piece in *Who's Irish?*, for each story provides an enlivening space for readers to inhabit.

CHAPTER 5

The Love Wife
Polyphonic Voices of the American Family

Gish Jen's third novel marks a departure in Jen's narrative style since *The Love Wife* (2004) is told from the first-person perspective of each member of the Wong family: wife Janie, née Bailey, who is referred to in the text as "Blondie" (a nickname given to her nonaffectionately by her mother-in-law, Mama Wong, who is not happy that her son married a white woman); husband Carnegie; adopted Asian American daughters Lizzy and Wendy; and Lanlan (or Lan), a relative of Mama Wong who comes from China to the United States to live with Carnegie and his family.[1] Whereas in all of Jen's previous novels and short stories the narrative voice stayed focalized through a single narrator (whether exterior to the action of the plot—heterodiegetic—or interior to the action of the narrative—homodiegetic), *The Love Wife* presents a polyphonic perspective on the Wongs and their adjustment to life with Lan, a plot development that threatens the marriage between Blondie and Carnegie, complicates the children's connection with their Chinese heritage and American identity, and upsets the entire family's sense of coherence. According to the literary scholar Margaret Homans, "The novel scrambles the categories of authentic and inauthentic, removing the boundary between them and dizzyingly redistributing their assignments in counterintuitive, postmodern ways."[2] Most especially *The Love Wife* engages with questions of who constitutes family and the lengths to which people will go to preserve their sense of family, while the novel also explores themes pertinent to Asian American life, such as interracial marriage, mixed-race family formations, domestic and transnational adoption, and the pleasures and perils of assimilation.

In *The Love Wife,* Jen stylistically signals her polyphonic narrative by using an em-dash construction with an absence of quotation marks, similar to the style used to denote dialogue in "House, House, Home," one in which direct quotation and free indirect discourse blend together. In a review for the radio show *Fresh Air,* Maureen Corrigan noted that "Jen constructs *The Love Wife* as a series of retrospective testimonies. . . . Instead of feeling contrived, this distinctive structure makes the novel feel less written, more talky." Michiko Kakutani, writing for the *New York Times,* described the multiple first-person narration as "choral" and lauded Jen for creating "a story that also represents her most ambitious and emotionally ample work yet."[3] By contrast, in a different *New York Times* book review, Craig Seligman found the narration a failed contrivance, declaring the multiplicity of first-person perspectives to be "a terrible idea, and not just because it's distracting. For the first time, Jen's writing is bland and unremarkable. In striving to create credible voices for her characters, she's abandoned her own."[4] While it is clear that critics do not share a consensus in their views about the diverse narrative voices, these show a stylistic innovation and a distinct shift in storytelling from her previous novels, one that the literary scholar Cynthia Callahan has astutely observed "possesses qualities of a documentary, as if some characters were addressing a silent audience located just off camera. Laid out like a play, the novel signals the character's point-of-view by introducing it with the speaker's name."[5] In a coauthored essay the scholars Fu-Jen Chen and Su-lin Yu relate, "In an interview, Jen herself explains that 'the novel came to me this way—as if told by the various Wongs at a very long family therapy session, only without the therapist,'" which is perhaps an apt description of *The Love Wife* since it does feel as though readers are listening in on this family's private confessions.[6]

The novel is told retrospectively by different members of the Wong family to an unnamed audience in an unmarked future. The event that the narrative hinges on is the arrival of Lanlan, who may or may not be the titular "love wife" alluded to in the novel. When Lan arrives in Boston's Logan Airport, it is 1999; Blondie is forty-five, Carnegie is thirty-nine, Lizzy is fifteen, Wendy is nine, Bailey is thirteen months, and Lan is a year older than Blondie but looks half her age—as Carnegie describes her, "No gray, and nary a wrinkle, thanks to that Asian predisposition toward subcutaneous fat. You could easily have taken her for a slightly older cousin of the girls."[7] In the logic of the narrative, it would seem that these disparate narrators are all in the same space when they describe the various aspects of Lan's arrival in the Wong home, since remarks that one character makes are often referenced by a subsequent character, sometimes as if the characters are engaged in a present-time dialogue about their recollections of past events, as when Blondie explains the couple's infertility issues:

> BLONDIE / We tried and tried.
> WENDY / Nobody wanted me exactly. Really they wanted their own baby. I was their second choice.
> BLONDIE / Not true!
> CARNEGIE / Second choice didn't mean second best.[8]

This exchange is an interlude to the story that the family tells about how Wendy came into their family—it is a flashback that interrupts the retrospective story that the family is trying to tell about Lan.

In other cases the multiple narrations form part of a running commentary, not necessarily in dialogue with one another but as a counterpoint to the narrative offered by different family members, as the example below describing Wendy and Lizzy's interpretation of Lan's newness to the United States demonstrates. Describing Lan's reaction to being in America, Wendy and Lizzy engage in a narrative that frames Lan as the wide-eyed foreigner intimidated by the largesse of the United States, but Lan's own narration undercuts this belief when Wendy discusses Lan's first trip to a grocery store:

> [WENDY /]—The grocery store is like that even in the winter.
>   In the winter too! she says.
> LIZZY / It's like she's surprised but embarrassed that she's surprised.
> LAN / *I did not go to university, but I was not ignorant.*[9]

Lan's rejoinder becomes a counternarrative to the story that Lizzy and Wendy create about her as a naive third-world immigrant. Additionally the italic type in Lan's narrative voice signals that she is speaking in Mandarin rather than English, a stylistic throwback from Jen's first novel, *Typical American,* which also employed italics to mark speech rendered in Chinese so that Jen could have her characters speaking fluidly rather than in stilted pidgin English.

The Love Wife is divided into two parts. Part 1 opens with a first chapter simply titled "Lan Arrives," which introduces us to Blondie, whose first sentence alerts us to the future tensions that will be explored: "The day Lan came, you could still say whose family this was—Carnegie's and mine."[10] Embedded in this opening is the sense of belonging—of Blondie's belief in closing off the boundaries of the family to the threat of an outsider. It also begs the question about how individual members feel themselves as belonging to a family, particularly when issues of race, ethnicity, and adoption are intertwined. Unlike Jen's previous novels, in which issues of race and identity unfold over the course of the narratives, *The Love Wife* proclaims these concerns immediately.

Blondie describes their family by noting, "We had three children. Two beautiful Asian girls—or should I say Asian American . . . both adopted; and one bio-boy Bailey, age thirteen months. Carnegie's ancestry being Chinese, and mine European, Bailey was half half, as they say—or is there another term by now?"[11] Blondie's self-conscious semicorrections about the racial identities of her children both illustrate her character type and announce the novel's interest in exploring the interracial and interethnic dynamics in this blended and mixed American family.

The story of Lan's immersion in the Wong household will span two years, though the Wongs and Lan will take detours in the telling of this story through various analepses to their past lives throughout part 1: to Carnegie's adoption of Lizzy; to Carnegie and Blondie's wedding; to Wendy's adoption in China; to Mama Wong's death; to Lan surviving China's Cultural Revolution; and to the circumstances that have led Lan to become a nanny for the Wong children. In the last chapter of part 1, "Time," readers learn that Mama Wong has left a will, unbeknownst to her only son, Carnegie, and in this will, which is in the possession of a Hong Kong relative, she has bequeathed a family book containing records of the Wong family to Wendy, "the only real Chinese in the family, as she called her."[12] However, before the book can be sent from Hong Kong to the United States, Carnegie and Blondie must agree to sponsor a relative of Mama Wong, Lanlan, to come to the United States and raise the children, so that, in the words of Mama Wong's will, "the children will at least speak Chinese, not like Carnegie."[13]

Carnegie, grief stricken over his mother's death and desperate for knowledge of his Chinese lineage, since he has only his nuclear, chosen family in the United States, desires the book and agrees to these conditions. Blondie, who was with Mama Wong (the subject of much of the penultimate chapter of part 1, "Carnegie Takes a Day Off") when she died and feels guilt stricken, agrees but believes that these conditions were meant to create a wedge in their family: "Only your mother, I said, would send us, from her grave, the wife you should have married."[14] This is another tension explored in the story: not simply Mama Wong's disapproval that Carnegie married a non-Chinese woman or that they had adopted children, only one of whom seems to be "pure" Chinese (Wendy was adopted from China, whereas Lizzy was left on a church doorstep in the Midwest), but the idea of choosing one's family—through marriage, through adoption—versus the ties of blood kinship that Mama Wong, Lan, and the biological son, Bailey, represent.

Of course Bailey as a mixed-race white-Asian child also adds to the complexity of the Wong family because his birth (detailed in the first half of chapter 8, "Carnegie Takes a Day Off") came so late in Blondie's life, during her early forties at a time when she had thought she was infertile, and because blond-haired Bailey favors his mother's side of the family. This fact secretly pleases Blondie, who says, "I was surprised what it meant to me, not to find my blood, my side, myself drowned out,"[15] and worries Carnegie, who confesses, "I worried that he would marry a white woman, like his daddy. I worried that no one in the delivery room would even be shocked if his child was born blond."[16] Underneath their pride and concern over Bailey's appearance is the idea that racial phenotype connotes belonging—to have your child physically resemble you, racially, means that your child is connected to you and your family heritage, as Blondie confirms: "The more I looked at him, the more I saw bits of my grandparents and parents, and all my brothers and sisters. Of course, he was Carnegie's son too—no one forgot that. And we completely loved the girls, just the same."[17] Prior to Bailey's birth, Blondie was the solo blond in their family, with Carnegie matching the girls. As Wendy notes, "Dad's parents were Chinese Chinese, like from China, so he has the same kind of skin as me and Lizzy."[18] Named Ellison Bailey Wong but always called Bailey in honor of his mother's side of the family, this mixed-race child of Carnegie and Blondie does not look "soup du jour"—the phrase that the Wongs use to describe people of multiracial or multiethnic heritage, for example Lizzy—and therefore both Blondie and Carnegie must reassure themselves of Carnegie's entitlement to call Bailey his "son too."

Furthermore, as Blondie's comments above about the girls make clear, she wants the unnamed audience to know that her love for Bailey is not greater than her love for her daughters. Yet the insertion of the last sentence, "And we completely loved the girls, just the same," particularly the phrase "just the same" to imply that they are the same as Bailey regardless of their nonbiogenetic status or their lack of resemblance to Blondie, undermines her intentions not to draw attention to the difference in her feelings toward her children. Indeed Blondie opines throughout part 1 that she loves the girls unconditionally, but such pronouncements are often accompanied, as in the above quote, with a contrast or a simile. Jen allows for Blondie's self-congratulatory comments to undercut her belief that her love is the same for her adopted daughters. Describing the pride she takes in parading around town with the girls, a white mother of two Asian children, Blondie asserts, "I had had the heart to take these children in, after all. Had I not loved them deeply and well, as if they were from the beginning my own?"[19] Again relying on a language of possession, Jen, using her character's first-person narration against Blondie, demonstrates the unspoken tension in Blondie's comments, namely that she does not actually think of Lizzy and Wendy as her daughters but "as if" they were hers—the simile drawing attention to the fact that they are not in actuality her daughters.

Yet Jen does not depict Blondie as a hypocritical monster of a mother. She is instead a fleshed-out and flawed person, one who loves her family, including her adopted daughters, even if she expresses herself imperfectly, betraying biases in the process. In the novel's first half we see glimpses into Carnegie and Blondie's past and the extraordinary affection they feel for one another and their children. Chapter 4, "A Family Is Born," chronicles the beginning of the Wong family when Carnegie was an electrical engineering graduate student in an unnamed midwestern college town. An "Oriental baby" (in the words of the nun who finds her) was found on a church doorstep, and as the only Asian adult in the town, Carnegie is enlisted to help.[20] Holding the baby for the first time, Carnegie develops an instant connection with little Lizzy. Holding her also coincides with the first time he meets Jane (soon to be renamed "Blondie"), who is visiting her friend Nomie Pierce, a doctor who is helping with the baby. Jane and Carnegie thus meet and fall in love at the same time that Carnegie meets and falls in love with Lizzy. Carnegie decides to adopt the baby, which is improbably granted, since in the real world single men are usually not granted custody of children, but as Jen via Carnegie explains, "the church was handling the placement, and there was racial compatibility to consider. 'Matching,' they called it."[21] Lizzy and Carnegie match racially, and yet the parents seem to agree, privately if not publicly, that Lizzy's ethnic makeup is "soup du jour" (a term Lizzy applies to herself throughout the novel and that other Wong members use as well), with Carnegie wondering, "Was she part Japanese? Part Korean? Part Vietnamese? Was she any part Chinese at all? Who knew?"[22]

Although Carnegie and Blondie do not know Lizzy's specific Asian ancestry, they do pursue an adoption in China for their second daughter, because as Blondie observes, it is "nice to have the children match."[23] Just as Carnegie is approved for his adoption of Lizzy due to his racial similarity, so too matching governs the Wongs' choice of a second adoption; in order to make Lizzy match with a sibling, they must go outside the United States to an Asian nation, particularly because Asian American children are not often put up for adoption in the United States.[24] Chapter 6, "Wendy," tells the story of how the Wong trio of Carnegie, Blondie, and Lizzy travel to China to adopt baby Wendy, which culminates in not only Wendy's adoption but also a harrowing experience while they are leaving the orphanage in which their hired car gets flipped over by an angry mob when their driver hits a pedestrian who turns out to be a textile worker laid off from a nearby factory. In this scene, which is not necessary for the plot of either the chapter or the novel, Jen's trademark sense of humor is on display. While the scene would be frightening as a real-life experience, in Jen's hands it plays out comically (with no fictional people being harmed in this scene, aside from the man who is hit by the car), particularly in the climactic moment of the car being turned over. As Carnegie narrates, "Lizzy popped up through a window as if from the hatch of a submarine, cradling the baby with her good arm.—She's making my arm hot! she cried. For her part, Wendy, astoundingly, had fallen asleep. Her hair bow was askew but still affixed to her fuzzy head."[25] Depicted as survivors rather than victims, with the almost cartoonish image of little Lizzy emerging as if from an aquatic adventure, the girls leave this scene unscathed, although "Lizzy insisted she was never ever going back to China. Nothing traumatic could be recounted without Lizzy putting in, *You think that's bad, you won't believe what happened in China.*"[26] Carnegie and Blondie originally plan this trip with six-year-old Lizzy in order to expose her to Chinese culture—even though they acknowledge that this may not even be the heritage of her ethnic ancestry. Yet as Jen shows by having the Wongs end up in a mob scene, the connection they desire for their oldest daughter goes horribly, if comically, awry, making the not so subtle point that connects with the theme of this novel: that your ideas of ancestry and family may not link up in the ways that you expect or want them to.

Nowhere is the disappointment of family more in evidence than in Mama Wong's attempts to prevent Carnegie and Blondie from marrying, which occurs eleven months after their first meeting. The wedding ceremony takes place in northern Maine on the Bailey family vacation property that they dub Independence Island (although they acknowledge that in truth it is a peninsula, since there is an earth access to the mainland). Locals, however, refer to it as Buck's Island in honor of Mr. Buck—the man who built the buildings on the island, a former boy's school that now serves as the vacation home for members of the Bailey clan, Blondie's brothers and sisters from Wisconsin and her father, a widowed doctor. The beach on the island, which locals call Sue's Beach after Mr. Buck's great-granddaughter, is used by the townfolk when the Bailey family is not in town (which is most of the year) and will serve as the site for the climactic events in part 2. In chapter 4, "A Family Is Born," the island is rendered as an idyllic family space for Carnegie and Blondie's union, with the one dissenting voice in the form of Mama Wong, who draws Carnegie and Blondie aside separately and offers each one (unbeknownst to the other) a million dollars to call off the wedding. Mama Wong cannot bear for her only son to be joined to Blondie and her family, not only because Blondie is white or because she is six years older than Carnegie but also because she believes the Bailey family to be on the decline: "They are not go up. They are go down. . . . In America people do not want anything, do not work hard, they are go down."[27] For Mama Wong, the Baileys' lack of ambition and relative prosperity signal their downward mobility, which she wants Carnegie to steer clear of, but Carnegie, not heeding his mother's advice or bribes, marries Blondie.

Besides showing how the Wong family came into being, part 1 also provides a backstory for Lan as well as a description of her life in America as the Wongs' nanny. Knowing only that she has been sponsored by the son of a distant relative to travel to the United States, Lan comes over on a student visa, takes classes at a local community college at night, and cares for the three Wong children by day. Chapter 3, "Automatica," chapter 5, "Nothing's Plenty for Me," and chapter 7, "A Kind of Guest" detail Lan's life with the Wongs interspersed with her Chinese anecdotes and an extended seven-page monologue detailing Lan's life in China: her mother's abandonment of their family when she ran away with an officer in the People's Army (Lan is told by her father that her mother died, later, due to a brain tumor); her father's former life as a principal of a small high school, where he was fluent in English, French, and Russian and also played the violin; their life being struggled against during the Cultural Revolution due to her father's previous education and class background; her father's murder by a Red Guard who accused him of not clapping loudly enough during a procommunist opera; Lan's time in a reeducation in the North being trained to fight against China's foes; her TB and her life with a great-aunt who nurses her back to health; her work in a shoe factory; her life as a migrant worker after the shoe factory closes; and the death of her great-aunt, which allows Lan to go to the United States without feeling that she has abandoned her. Some of the details that Jen uses in Lan's monologue are echoed in "Duncan in China," particularly the description of being struggled against, although in Lan's monologue it is more grisly, desperate, and grim: there are no humorous asides to leaven the brutality of Lan's life, which seems to be a fictional representation for the countless real people who suffered during the Cultural Revolution.

Although Lan bonds with the children and is polite with Carnegie, she keeps Blondie at arm's length, not trusting her and interpreting Blondie's gestures as hostile rather than generous. For example, Blondie tells us that she installed Lan in the bedroom apartment above the garage (a former converted barn that is still used to house a pet goat, Tommy, on the bottom floor) because she thought Lan would want privacy. But Lan interprets (perhaps not so inaccurately) that staying outside the main house is a way of keeping Lan from being a real member of the family—she is a distant relative, with the emphasis on distant, and she is there not out of the generosity and charity of Carnegie and Blondie but because they are responding to the edicts of Mama Wong's will in order to obtain the Wong family book. Initially they do not tell Lan why they have asked her to come to the United States: "*Why was I brought here? Because Carnegie's mother wanted me to come, they said. But I wondered, what was the real reason? What did they want from me?*"[28] But in the first candid conversation between Carnegie and Lan, which is also where Carnegie reveals his developing attraction to her, Carnegie tells her about the will, which still makes Lan ask him, "But why your mother want me to come here?," a question he cannot answer until the family book makes its fateful appearance in the novel's last chapter.[29]

Part 1 features a loose chronology of Lan's arrival and settling into the Wong household, but its main purpose is to offer various flashbacks that flesh out the backstory of each narrator and how he or she became a part of the Wong New England homestead. By contrast, part 2 provides a more straightforward chronology of the Wongs and the cataclysmic events that result from Lan's arrival, with the first four chapters depicting the prosaic day-to-day experiences of the family as they adjust to life with Lan, particularly focusing on Blondie. In chapter 10, "Trying to Be Happy," Blondie expresses what turns out to be a self-fulfilling prophecy—that Lan will usurp her place in her home. Although Carnegie continually reassures her, "Our family will always be our family. . . . And you will always be my Blondie," Blondie writes to her best friend, Gabriela, on e-mail and tells her, "The girls are no longer quite mine" and recounts comments they have made about feeling a stronger connection with Lan and Lizzy's telling her that "she honestly wouldn't be surprised to find out Lan was her real mother."[30] Feeling threatened by Lan's closeness to her daughters, Blondie reaches out to each of them: she tries to assuage Wendy's anxieties over a classmate who has been tormenting her at school and to reassure Lizzy that it is OK for her to be the only soup du jour kid in her class and to not know her ethnic makeup. Blondie's advice to ignore the kids in school speaks to her white privilege and lack of understanding for what her Asian adopted daughter is going through. Lizzy challenges Blondie's assertion that she is "soup du jour, too" because she is German, Scotch, Irish, and American, telling her, "Yeah, but it doesn't matter as much because you're white and not adopted. Nobody wonders where you're from, nobody asks you."[31] Although Blondie does not seem to be able to relate to her teenage daughter, Lan finds a connection to both girls through their shared orphan status, telling them, "I am like you, have no real mother. Have no real family."[32]

Although Blondie's fear and anxiety about Lan prior to her arrival may have been premature, Lan's continual dismissal of Blondie and comments, such as the above, to the girls that they have no real mother and thus no real family undermine Blondie's attempts, at this moment, to connect with her daughters and reinforce a belief that adopted families are somehow not real families— that the girls are for all intents and purposes motherless children living with a fake mother who Lan believes also to be a phony. Deciding to concentrate on improving her relationship with Lan, Blondie begins taking cooking lessons from her in chapter 11, "A Happy Family," and indeed, as the title suggests, members of the family seem to form a new bond over the Chinese food that Lan teaches Blondie to cook, with Carnegie observing that "Blondie seemed bent on normalizing her relationship with Lan through foodstuffs."[33] Yet despite the newfound contentment or détente at their dinner table, Blondie's anxiety and unease at Lan's presence in their midst manifest at Carnegie's fortieth birthday party when she looks in the dining room mirror and realizes that the racial difference she feels from her family became exacerbated with Lan's arrival. Blondie imagines that "if I thought about this being the group that would gather around my deathbed . . . I thought of myself as dying abroad—in the friendly bosom of some foreign outpost."[34] In this revelation, as in her previous candid remarks about loving the girls "as if" they were her own, Blondie's racial and ethnic biases come out as she reduces her Asian American family members to foreigners, a particularly pernicious stereotype that Asian Americans have had to fend off, their Asian difference being a mark that prevents people from seeing them as fully enfranchised American citizens.

After the birthday party, Blondie is increasingly troubled by feeling like an outsider in her own family. In chapter 12, "Blondie Takes a Day Off," Blondie comes home after spending a day with her best friend, Gabriela, who is newly returned from abroad, to discover her family sitting at the dinner table working on various projects and homework assignments and observes, "How much more natural this scene than the one that included me."[35] Again, Blondie concentrates on the visual similarity of her Asian American family members, and also Lan, and interprets this racial similarity to be "natural," thus implying that mixed-race families are somehow unnatural, perverse, or unreal. Fearing that she is being replaced by Lan, Blondie decides to quit her high-powered corporate job and stay home so that she can spend more time with her children, even though Carnegie tells her, "You don't have to do this to get the family back."[36] Yet his very admission that she has lost control of the family signals that Blondie's decision is an important step in reconnecting with her daughters and laying claim to the family in light of Lan. Chapter 13, "Blondie Quits," describes Blondie's new life as a stay-at-home mother who takes the girls to museums and plays, drives the children to the beach to build sandcastles, and immerses herself in her garden. Her jealousy over Lan, however, spills over into fury when she discovers Lan napping with Bailey. She angrily tells Carnegie, "She already has the girls, she cannot have Bailey too . . . I want my home back. . . . Where this is my house, and these are my children, I get to decide what the rules are. I get to decide who sleeps with who."[37] Given Blondie's previous remarks about feeling a distinct sense of kinship with Bailey due to his resemblance to her, Lan's cuddling up with baby Bailey strikes a particular chord of resentment in Blondie. When she and Carnegie send an e-mail to the Hong Kong relative titled "Returning Lan Now," he responds by telling them that he cannot give them the family book unless Lan remains with them for at least two years.

Seeking a different solution to the Lan problem, Blondie introduces her to Shang (whose name is also the title of chapter 14), whom Gabriela once dated and whom Blondie has met in a feng shui class. Lan describes him as being a man "*a little older than me—in his fifties—and* [who] *called himself Shang, after his grandfather, who came from Fujian. I think his real name was Brian. He did not look Chinese at all. Not even as Chinese as Bailey, just like any lao wai, brown hair all over.*"[38] Shang's introduction into their lives will set off a series of events that will have devastating consequences for the entire family. But initially he is the answer to both Blondie's problem with Lan and Lan's loneliness. Shang is the kind of person who professes to love all things Chinese and who has traveled to Taiwan and the mainland. From there he brought back with him a man, Su Jiabao, a former professor who now works as his chauffeur in the United States. Shang's interest in Lan is both romantic and professional: he wants her to be his business partner and Chinese cultural liaison in an on-line gambling business venture he wants to start up in Suzhou, China, Lan's hometown. With Shang, Lan becomes a new person, wearing makeup, dressing in more revealing and expensive clothes (compliments of Shang), and spending more time with him and less time with the children. However, this new business-romantic venture does not come without costs. Shang, still married with children, insists on picking Lan up behind the town's post office rather than at the Wong home so as to avoid being seen with her by the neighbors, and Carnegie and Blondie begin to notice rips and tears in Lan's new clothing, along with cuts and bruises on her body.

As the fighting between Shang and Lan increases, Lan finds herself more and more in the company of Shang's chauffeur, a fellow Chinese immigrant who is now a naturalized citizen. Su grew up in a village close to Suzhou and starts spending more time with Lan in her barn apartment. Lan and Su develop a friendship and budding romance, facilitated by Su's dropping Lan off at home after her nights with Shang. Discovering that Su has been spending time with Lan, Shang drives over one day in a jealous rage. Looking for Lan in the barn, Shang is accosted and head butted by Tommy, Gabriela's pet goat that the Wongs keep for her on their property. Briefly redirecting his rage at Tommy, Shang takes a pitchfork from the toolshed next to the garage and stabs Tommy until he is bleeding and then dead in the yard. Unable to stop Shang from killing Tommy, Lan finds herself accused of being a whore and having her clothes ripped off her by Shang, whose rage seems fueled rather than abated from killing the goat. Wendy, who has observed everything from her perch atop a nearby tree, jumps down when Shang starts ripping off Lan's clothes and tells him to leave Lan alone. Lan, attempting to protect Wendy, tells her, "It's a game. I like it. . . . Really. You don't have to worry," as Shang drags Lan into the garage.[39] Grabbing the pitchfork from the toolshed, Wendy goes into the garage and rescues a now nearly naked Lan by hitting Shang with the pitchfork twice, while Lan escapes his grip and attacks him until he lies on the ground moaning, thus bringing chapter 14 to a close.

The violence at the end of chapter 14 is where the narrative shifts into high gear, as increasingly various developments will commence in what one reviewer has called "hokey plot high jinks," as the novel pivots from documenting the domestic elements of the Wong family to incidents and events of a more catastrophic nature.[40] Carnegie's narration begins chapter 15, "Independence Island," by explaining that in order to protect Lan, given her noncitizen status, they do not press charges against Shang; instead they send her, along with Su, to Independence Island, the Baileys' vacation home. Blondie's father, Doc Bailey, had given the island/peninsula to Blondie and Carnegie as a wedding gift (with the consent of her siblings), and now Carnegie and Blondie offer it as a refuge to Lan and Su while Shang cools down. With Lan no longer enrolled in classes, she and Su marry so that she can apply for a green card since Su is a naturalized American citizen. The first thing they do in Maine is open up a storefront selling Chinese food, with dumplings that become so popular that people stand in long lines for them and a local newspaper article heralds Lan and Su's business savvy. Meanwhile, back in Massachusetts, the Wongs settle into life without Lan: they find a therapist for Wendy to help her cope with the traumatic events involving Shang; Lizzy breaks up with her musician boyfriend Russell after a brief stint of moving in with him and then starts dating her old reliable (and parent-approved) boyfriend Derek; Carnegie gets a new job at a nonprofit that makes him happier; Blondie cooks and enjoys three blissful seasons of having her family to herself; and Bailey begins to talk.

However, as spring turns to summer, trouble brews for Lan and Su. First, their business becomes so popular that they need to expand, causing them to rent a more expensive storefront. This propels them to fire the local help and hire Chinese immigrant workers (one legal and one not so legal) to bring down costs, but Su and Lan lie and tell people that these new workers are related to Su. When the locals find out that the new workers are not skilled family employees but just cheaper immigrant laborers, they complain, causing Lan and Su to fire the Chinese help and rehire their local staff. But the damage has been done, and the townspeople begin to grumble about Lan and Su's clannishness, to question their trustworthiness, and to accuse them of bias, since some customers, particularly their African American clientele, believe that they are receiving fewer dumplings in their bags than are given to other customers. Rumors also fly about the use of peanut oil, which one mother says caused her child to be hospitalized due to a nut allergy, and the locals also begin to misquote Lan and Su from the newspaper article. Lan and Su told the reporter that the reason their business is successful is because they work hard, but when all the grumblings about Lan and Su occur, the locals misremember the quote as Lan and Su claiming that the reason they succeed is because they work harder than anyone else. Thus Lan and Su become reinterpreted and reviled as smug immigrants who believe the local townspeople to be lazy failures.

In this hostile atmosphere Lan and Su find themselves additionally targeted in the summer months when the trailer park inhabitants take up residence on the island's beach, which the locals believe belongs to Sue, the great-granddaughter of Mr. Buck, the peninsula's original owner. Buck bequeathed the land and buildings to the boys' school, which in turn sold it to the Baileys over a generation ago. Chapter 16, "Sue's Beach," commences with one last backtrack by Carnegie that will explain the tragic events that befall Su and Lan. In chapter 8, "Carnegie Takes a Day Off," Carnegie drives up to Maine to check on the Bailey property. There he encounters the trailer park residents on the beach and meets Sue Buck, who is squatting in one of the guest cottages along with her toddler daughter, Ashley. He invites mother and daughter to dine with him and ascertains that Sue is homeless, mentally ill, and a smoker, as he has to stomp on a cigarette butt that she carelessly throws on the ground next to the main house. Returning to the main story about Lan and Su, we next learn that they too have encountered Sue Buck, who walked unannounced into their bedroom one summer night. Sue believes that the island is her home and that the Baileys have no right of ownership since her great-grandfather left it for the school and the town's children and not for a private owner, particularly an outsider not from Maine. Sue is supported by the other townspeople who use the beach, especially when sometime in July, Su tries to shoo away the beachgoers to prevent them from building bonfires near his home, to which one vocal local challenges his property rights by saying, "You must admit there's something wrong with [the Baileys] giving it to foreigners to use when the people who live here have no beach whatsoever."[41] When Su challenges him and tells him that he is not a foreigner but an American citizen, the local uses the illogic of xenophobic jingoism, telling Su, "A citizen thinks this country is about law. But an American knows it is about who is really American."[42]

Lan intervenes before things can escalate, and the next morning she departs for a doctor's appointment, leaving Su asleep in their bed. When she leaves the doctor's office, she is in shock because he has just told her that she is three months pregnant, a seeming impossibility for the forty-seven-year-old Lan. Yet what she soon discovers when she looks up at the sky is even more shocking and ultimately devastating, because the island has been engulfed in flames. Su has died, asphyxiated by the smoke (as is soon surmised at the funeral home given the peaceful look on his face) from the fire that burned every building on the island, a fire that some believe may have been caused by an errant bonfire left burning on the beach or by Sue accidently (or maliciously?) setting it off during one of her nightly excursions. While a cause for the fire is never determined, the tragedy foments a change among the locals, who leave flowers and a rock on which a heart with the word "Su" in the middle is drawn, thus renaming the beach "Su's beach" in his honor.

The final chapter, "The Waiting Room," features more shake-ups in the Wongs' world. Readers discover that the pregnant Lan has moved back in with the Wongs and this time is staying in the main house, while Blondie has moved out in protest, telling the girls that she wants time to figure out her relationship with their father. The girls accuse her of abandoning them, especially since she takes Bailey with her to her new cottage. Meanwhile Lan has assumed the duties of cooking and caring for the children, which leads one morning to the consummation of the mutual attraction between Lan and Carnegie, even though Carnegie later professes his love for Blondie and his desire for her to return home.

With Carnegie and Blondie's relationship at an impasse, Lan pregnant and sexually entangled with Carnegie, and the girls shuttling between two homes, the family book finally arrives in the mail from the Hong Kong relative. Revealed in his note, written in English so that Carnegie can read and understand its shocking and disturbing implications, is that the family book "is the story of your mother's family, going back 17 generations in Sichuan. Of course, she is the first generation where we write down the girls, lucky she is in it. Unfortunately, you are not in it, because you were adopted in the United States. Anyway you were not born yet when the book was updated. However your older sister will be happy to see her name, the only child in her whole generation."[43] In just three sentences Carnegie's entire life is overturned as he first learns that he is the adopted son of Mama Wong and that Lan is his older sister—the one who believed that her mother had died of a brain tumor, since this is what her father had told her when in reality her mother had abandoned her for an army officer. Finding the textual proof of her name recorded inside the family book, Lan tries to reassure Carnegie that at least he is not her real brother, thus making their intercourse not a matter of incest. However, Carnegie, disturbed not only at the implications of his relations with Lan but also at his newfound status as an adoptee, has a heart attack and is rushed into emergency surgery.

While he is in the hospital Carnegie has a reverie involving Mama Wong in which he questions her about his adoption, about Lan, about why she failed to tell him that he was adopted or that Lan was his sister, and about his realization that "I love Blondie . . . I married the love wife."[44] The last words that Carnegie's narration leaves readers with are a command by Mama Wong to "Go! Go!" and indeed it seems he has heeded her instruction since members of his family are given the good news in the waiting room that he has recovered.[45] Greeting this news with cheers and hugs, Blondie, Lan, Wendy, Lizzy, and Bailey are united in their relief that Carnegie is alive. However, the novel ends on an ambiguous note as Blondie and Lan let go of each other and Wendy has the last words of the narrative: "It's amazing how dark a room can suddenly get."[46] Yes, Carnegie will survive, but as Wendy explains, "Yet we know now, too, what we know." What they know is that Lan is in her second trimester, the newly discovered sister of the newly discovered adopted Carnegie, and Blondie is still living in a cottage with Bailey, away from the girls, who now share with their father the adoptee mantra that being second choice does not mean being second best.[47] Jen closes the narrative on this ambivalent image in order to recognize that while the novel ends on a hopeful note with Carnegie's recovery, it is unclear whether the Wongs will ever recover from the things they now know about one another.

CHAPTER 6

World and Town
Growing Old in a Global New World Order

Gish Jen's fourth and most recent novel, *World and Town* (2010), focuses mainly on sixty-eight-year-old, biracial (half white, half Chinese) Hattie Kong, a recently widowed and retired high school biology teacher, although two other characters, Sophy and Everett, receive chapters of their own. Hattie had moved to Riverlake two years before the time the novel opens, and she is still mourning for her husband, Joe, and her best friend, Lee—back-to-back deaths. The arrival of her ex-lover and former lab mentor Carter Hatch and a Cambodian immigrant-exiled family propels Hattie into dramas both big (arson, child abuse, suicide) and small (the death of a pet, serving as cultural ambassador, contentious town hall meetings). As the novel's title suggests, the actions and preoccupations of Hattie are of a global and local scale, as various members of Riverlake and Hattie's diasporic Chinese extended family make demands on her. Yet as readers come to realize by the last pages of the novel, the world and town of the novel's title are neither distant nor unrelated entities; nor is one a small-scale version contained within the other. Instead *World and Town*, through its themes of loss, rebirth, identity, and community, illustrates the universal commonalities that humans share through the distinct differences in their unique life experiences.[1]

Most importantly *World and Town* demonstrates the evolution of Jen's maturing prose voice, particularly through her grieving and aging heroine, Hattie, a portrait of growing old that is graceful and subtly moving. As the reviewer Ron Charles of the *Washington Post* observed, *World and Town* is "another in a small but growing collection of books about getting older—not getting decrepit or sick or depressed, but just getting older, with all the perspective such maturity can endow."[2] Indeed this is the most mature protagonist in Jen's novels to date, in terms of both age and thoughtful retrospection. While Jen has previously written about older characters, such as Mama Wong in *The Love Wife,* the unnamed Chinese immigrant mother in "Who's Irish?," and an elderly Chinese man in the short story "Amaryllis," this is the first time she presents us with an elderly Chinese American protagonist, one who is fluent in both Chinese and English and who is not undergoing the conflicts of becoming an American, for she has already accomplished this by the age of sixty-eight. Hattie Kong realizes that she has fewer days ahead of her than behind her, and Jen presents her as a fully fleshed-out character who is rendered neither comically nor tragically but simply as a woman living her life as a retired widow in a small New England town.

World and Town offers a mature prose voice not simply because Hattie is sixty-eight but because it demonstrates the development of Jen as a fiction writer, as someone who has polished her craft for over twenty years and experimented with different character perspectives and voices and various innovative narrative constructions. Jen's prose in *World and Town* reflects her mastery as a fiction writer: the details she includes that are comic, beautiful, and haunting; the various plot strains that seem disconnected in the first chapter and that get woven together throughout the novel; and the philosophical questions that run as an undercurrent of introspection amid the plot's twists and turns. As the literary critic Min Song noted, "Gish Jen's characteristic style, honed to a sharp point in her earlier works, remains sharp, but in this most recent work, it has also gained a patina of hard-won wisdom, which in turn makes the prose more somber than cheerful."[3] Though *World and Town* offers up Jen's trademark humor, it is of a more subdued sort. As the *New York Times* reviewer Donna Rifkind has affirmed of the novel's darker tone, "Grief is all over, with a jittery undertone of suspicion; and the novel's humor, while plentiful, is most often edged in black."[4] One such moment occurs early in the novel when the heterodiegetic narrator describes Hattie's feelings over the deaths of her husband and her best friend: "Joe died and then Lee, in a kind of one-two Hattie still can't quite believe. It was like having twins; at one point they were even both in the recovery room together. She got to book the same church with the same pianist for both funerals, and did think she should have gotten some sort of twofer from the crematorium."[5] As this passage indicates, there are glimmers of amusement and humor in the sorrowful circumstances of Hattie's losses.

World and Town begins with a series of three epigraphs that foreshadow the larger concerns of the novel: one by Alexis de Tocqueville about the characteristics of an American; another by the scientists Neil Campbell and Jane Reece about vision as a relationship between the eye and the brain; and a final one by

the Buddha, who said, "With our thoughts, we make the world."⁶ Organized by
a prologue and five chapters, *World and Town* combines narrational elements
from Jen's past novels, employing a heterodiegetic narrator as her first two
did and relying on a choral technique similar to that in *The Love Wife* so that
readers are privy not only to the thoughts and actions of the protagonist Hattie
Kong but also to the backstories and perspectives of Sophy (pronounced So-
PEE) and Everett. Having Hattie's three focalized chapters interspersed with a
chapter on Sophy and another on Everett creates the effect of hearing a community's story rather than just an individual's, which connects to the larger themes
of the novel about our actions and reactions impacting those in our community, whether in the small nuclear family or in the larger global world order.

The novel opens with a brief prologue, "A Lost World," that describes
Hattie's early life in China, giving us a biographical outline of her character
that will be fleshed out in the pages to follow: she is a sixty-eight-year-old
American citizen; she is the daughter of a white American missionary mother
and a Chinese father who was descended from Confucius, or Kŏngzi as he is
called in China; and she grew up in Qingdao, a cosmopolitan city known for
its German-inspired beer. Hattie recalls the Kong family cemetery in Qufu,
a place where only members of the male line (along with their wives) are al-
lowed to be buried, thus precluding Hattie (but not her brothers) from joining
her ancestors in their final resting place. The family graveyard is also a site of
desecration during the Cultural Revolution, as villagers rob the graves and take
the fertile earth for their farms. Hattie reflects back on her family plot because
having buried a husband and a best friend, she ponders where she should be
buried. She concludes that since her son is gallivanting around the world, her
three dogs are her closest companions and therefore, *"Maybe she should be
buried in the pet cemetery?"*⁷

Chapter 1, "Hattie I: I'll But Lie and Bleed Awhile," situates readers to a
time and place relevant to the focalization of its protagonist Hattie Kong. We
learn that "last week, a family moved in down the hill—Cambodian" and that
where we are is Riverlake, "a good town, an independent town—a town that
dates to before the Revolution. A town that was American before America was
American."⁸ Although we are never given a specific state that Riverlake resides
in, from the context clues we know it is somewhere in New England, most likely
Vermont since there are references to leaf peepers, mud rooms, no see-ums, and
sugar season.⁹ Independent Riverlake is a small town where residents like its
slow pace of life and define it against the urban center that it is nowhere near, as
a town hall meeting to discuss the building of a cell phone tower demonstrates.
The majority of the townspeople at the meeting do not support the tower (and
feel even more negatively toward the family who has sold the land to the cell

phone people), and as one local rhetorically says to the cell phone company's lawyer, "Whose town is this? . . . Not yours. No, sir. Not yours."[10] The question of whose town this is or rather whose home this is remains relevant throughout the novel as various characters must confront where they belong and whether the different spaces they once counted as home are truly theirs. Commenting on the themes of belonging and space, Jen's fellow creative writer Elizabeth Graver has observed that "Jen has always written beautifully about space and how it can serve as a container or crucible for her characters—the welfare hotel in 'Birthmates,' the array of houses in her long story 'House, House, Home'— but in *World and Town,* the containers and their contents are more varied, and the interrogation of the ideas of home and community, continuity and change, are both broader and deeper."[11] Where people call home and who makes up their community are central themes of the novel. Hattie, a two-year resident of Riverlake, moved there only after she retired. Once her husband and best friend, fellow teachers at the same high school, died, Hattie could no longer stand to walk onto the campus, and so she finds herself living in a two-bedroom cottage with a view of the lake and her new Cambodian neighbors. Riverlake is her new and perhaps last home, since the prologue opens on thoughts of her mortality.

Though Hattie is lonely, she does have her dogs to keep her company at home and her walking group to connect her to the town. She also has the new-found preoccupation of watching the Cambodian family settle into the trailer that sits below Hattie's house. She spies on them with her binoculars, noting their various movements and the improvements they are making to the trailer and the lot it sits on. Hattie's peeping, we learn, derives not from nosiness so much as loneliness. She desires connection, and through a neighborly bag of cookies and the gift of an old wheelbarrow, Hattie soon finds her distant spying replaced with actual interactions with this family, which consists of Ratanak Chhung, the patriarch; his wife, Mum, their teenage son, Sarun; and their adolescent daughter, Sophy, whom Hattie befriends through trips to the farmer's market, where she gifts Sophy with a bunch of early spring peonies. Hattie learns from Sophy about the Chhungs' life before Riverlake: that there are two daughters in foster care; that they came to this town in the north to restart their lives; and that the parents and Sarun are survivors of Pol Pot's genocidal regime, known in the United States as the Killing Fields. Details of the Chhungs' trauma will be divulged in the following chapter, but what is clear to Hattie as it is to readers is that the Chhung family is not thriving; they are barely surviving, as Sophy confirms to Hattie: "We've been here my whole life and still don't have anything because my dad can't work and if my mom isn't giving money to her brother, she's giving it to the temple."[12] Ratanak, a man barely able to speak English, suffers from PTSD and is forced to wear a back brace after he hurts himself digging a drainage ditch on the trailer lot. Mum, illiterate in both Khmer and English, cleans homes but also gives away her money, as Sophy says. These facts leave Sarun to be the breadwinner in the family, and though Hattie is not clear how he has money, from the things Sophy says, she conjectures that his gang activities provide him with money for the big-screen TV and food for their family.

There are two other distractions for Hattie in this opening chapter: her extended family's requests for the reburial of Hattie's parents and her reunion with Carter Hatch. Carter, who has recently returned to Riverlake, the place of his family's summer home, is a retired neuroscientist. He and Hattie confront their past rifts only to discover that the cause of their falling-out—Carter's failure to help promote Hattie's career—is not in the past; it is very much part of the present resentment that Hattie still feels toward Carter and is complicated by a brief romantic interlude they shared in college. Hattie's extended Chinese family bombards her with e-mail requests for the reburial of her parents to the ancestral graveyard. As Hattie is head of the family (both Hattie's younger brothers have passed), her nieces and nephews seek her permission to take their grandparents' remains from Iowa (where Hattie's mother's family hails from) back to Qufu. Believing that their family suffers from bad luck—an anorexic daughter, a schizophrenic son, and assorted financial and emotional difficulties—the Kongs believe that the feng shui of the grandparents in Iowa is bad and thus causes bad luck in the extended family. Only by returning their remains to the ancestral family plot will order be restored. For Hattie, these pleas signal the outdated and distinctly unmodern ideas that her scientific mind cannot support, and she politely but firmly writes back to her relatives, *"I'm so sorry to hear of your troubles, but do you really think moving the graves will help you?"*[13]

Like Hattie's relatives, the Chhungs believe in karma and fate and luck, their lives a series of both extreme fortune and misfortune. In chapter 2, "Sophy: How They Even Got Here," we learn just that: how the Chhungs got to Riverlake and how they got to be a family. Like Hattie's chapters, Sophy's employs heterodiegetic narration, but it is unclear whether this is the same omniscient narrator who has shared the thoughts and inner musings of Hattie. Sophy's narrator uses the same types of locutions and lingo that the fifteen-year-old Cambodian American girl does, as in this section where the narrator describes Sophy learning about Cambodia's various invasions: "The Thais came, and then the Cham, and then the Japanese—or maybe the Japanese were the Chinese? Anyway, it was hard for Sophy to understand. Like did they all just wake up one day and think, Let's invade Cambodia? Because it was wack, it really was, the way that, after that the French came and after that the Vietnamese and, like no one thought, Man, that is so copycat."[14] The omniscient narrator so closely matches Sophy's speech patterns and teenage slang—"like," "wack," "copycat"—that it is as if one of Sophy's friends is telling her story, a sympathetic teenage friend who knows all of the Chhungs' past history and all of Sophy's thoughts, regrets, hopes, and dreams.

Ratanak Chhung was a successful engineer in Cambodia married to a beautiful woman who was Chinese Cambodian like him. His younger brother married Mum, a woman from the country, whose family were successful farmers. When Pol Pot came into power, their respective families were torn apart: Chhung's brother was killed because the soldiers mistook him for Ratanak; Chhung's wife was killed for refusing to marry one of the Khmer Rouge; and Mum's sons died of starvation. After the war Sophy's parents were reunited in a Thai refugee camp, where they also found the son of Ratanak's sister, a baby they named Sarun. So the war killed off their original families and helped to create this new family: a brother and sister-in-law common-law married (Sophy explains their unofficial marriage to Hattie by referring to them as a camp couple) with an adopted son from their sister.

After the reunion and formation of this new family in the refugee camp, the narrator jumps forward to Sophy's teen years and the events that propelled their family out of their old home and into Riverlake. Sophy is living in an unnamed town with her parents, Sarun, her baby brother Gift (who is given this name because Mum believes he is the incarnation of her dead sons, who have returned to her as a gift in the form of this new baby boy), and her two younger sisters, Sopheap and Sophan. Although it is unclear where the city is located, it contains other Cambodian exiles and Southeast Asian refugees, such as Sophy's boyfriend Ronnie, a wannabe rock star who is not in a gang but does play gigs for the Crips.[15] Sophy runs away from home to live with Ronnie when they start having sex, but the police come for her, and in juvenile court she is disowned by her parents and forced to live with a foster family. While there she realizes that she is pregnant and then miscarries, which coincides with her discovery that her former boyfriend has a new girlfriend, leading her to run away back to her parents, who call the police so that she is next put in a group home. When she runs away a second time, again to see her parents, she learns that while she has been gone her sisters have both gotten involved with gangs and have been placed in separate foster homes. She also finds out that her father, while he was drunk, had dangled Gift out their window because the baby would not stop crying, and now neighbors threaten to report him for being an unfit parent.

Deciding that they all need a new life (and not wanting Sophy to be returned to the group home or Gift to be taken away), the Chhungs are sponsored by a local church to be relocated to Riverlake immediately, since the original Cambodian family who was supposed to move had changed their minds. After three bus transfers, the Chhungs arrive in their new home, where church members help them get situated, providing rides into town and giving them a trailer and a lot to live on. Their adjustment in Riverlake is not as difficult as they expected, especially because they are among the few "black-hairs" (the phrase used throughout *World and Town* to signal either people of color or Asians specifically) in town. Although the original church group who sponsored them refuses to help them any further when they realize that they are not Christian and that they are not even the original family meant to arrive in Riverlake, a different fundamentalist church, the Heritage Bible Church, steps in and offers assistance to the Chhungs, sending around a blue car to drive them into town for their errands. One day Sophy, who is watching Gift, gets into the blue car, and it takes them to the church and to Bible study. She befriends three girls her own age, all teens who have babies. The church offers toys for Gift and cookies for Sophy, along with material items that she can take back to her family and more immaterial but stronger enticements in the form of acceptance, community, and friendship. Soon she is being embraced by the church members and is confessing her past sins to them and being reborn as a Christian in their church, sponsored mainly by Hattie's walking group friend Ginny, whose religious zeal and relationship with Sophy will play a pivotal role later in the novel.

Sophy's chapter is designed mainly to give readers a greater understanding of the Chhungs: the extreme deprivation and violence they witnessed and lived through in Cambodia; the post-traumatic stress that trickles down from the parents to the children; the poverty and violence that are part of their lives in the United States; and the distinctiveness of their experiences. While several book reviewers have talked about the themes of immigration in *World and Town*, noting that both the Chhungs and Hattie are immigrants, this phrase cannot adequately or accurately capture the Chhungs' experience. They did not choose to leave their homeland; they did not immigrate to the United States for the American dream of upward mobility. They are exiles—refugees of war—and survivors of genocide. Chhung drinks and smokes and shouts at his family, while Mum prays at the Buddhist temple and gives their money away, always wanting to help others who seemingly have even less than they do. The Chhungs are not an immigrant success story, and they are not the Asian American model minority; instead the Chhungs are an example of people who live on the margins of society—who are holding on to what they have and surviving day by day because any day in the United States is better than the life they left in the Killing Fields.

Hattie too, as we will learn in chapter 3, "Hattie II: Rising to Fight Again," is an immigrant not out of choice but out of necessity. In one of two extended

analepses, the narrator flashes back to Hattie's life; the first finds her in post–
World War II China with the communist threat on the horizon. Hattie leaves
China by assuming the identity of a recently deceased adopted daughter of
fellow American missionaries and briefly lives with her maternal grandparents
in Iowa. Fearful of whether she will ever see her family or return to China,
Hattie is an exile rather than an immigrant, just like the Chhungs. She has not
chosen to come to the United States; she was made to do so out of parental
love and protection. Because her grandparents are too old to care for her, she is
sent to live with the friends of her anthropologist uncle Jeremy. He and his wife
Susan are unable to take care of Hattie because they are leaving for fieldwork
in Tanzania, so seventeen-year-old Hattie is sent to an unnamed city, where she
grows up with the Hatch family: the scientist Dr. Hatch; his wife; and their
three sons, Anderson, Carter, and Reedie. Bestowing the affectionate nickname
"Miss Confucius" on her, the Hatches try to make Hattie a part of their family,
but she, as an exiled half Chinese and half American girl who misses her family
and her homeland, finds herself *"just foreign—wàiláide. . . . A stranger."*[16]

Although Hattie learns to be comfortable with the Hatches, she never loses
the sense that she is an outsider. In the second extended analepsis, Hattie recounts her time with Carter while working in his lab. After one romantic colle-
giate weekend together, Hattie and Carter settle into a professional relationship
when she becomes a Ph.D. candidate under his tutelage since Carter achieved
his doctorate rapidly and has already risen in the ranks by having his own lab.
Although both Carter and Hattie are romantically attached to other people,
their closeness is palpable to most, particularly Dr. Hatch. Carter initially tells
Hattie that he will help her in her career advancement, but when a position
opens in his department (this after Hattie has graduated and pursued a post-
doctorate elsewhere), a jealous colleague accuses Carter of hiring his mistress.
When Carter then does nothing to defend either himself or Hattie, the job is
given to someone else. Hattie sees this as a betrayal of his promise to her as well
as a betrayal of his feelings for her.

Besides these two flashbacks, this second of Hattie's chapters propels the
plot forward along its different axes. Carter, who is now dating someone new,
is the town hero when he stands up to the Value-Mart lawyers and devises an
innovative plan to change the town's dumping fees for trucks to ten thousand
dollars, effectively making the town an unattractive site for the megastore.
Ginny, the woman who has befriended Sophy at church, has kicked her husband Everett out of their home after thirty-seven years of marriage because
Everett refuses to be born again into the Heritage Bible Church. Sophy's growing religiosity and fervor set her against her non-Christian family and Hattie,

especially when Hattie tries to talk to Sophy about her faith and tells her that being Christian does not mean having to turn away from her family. In addition a mysterious white van appears in town, which Sarun enters and then disappears for days at a time. This leaves the townspeople and his parents wondering where he goes and what he is doing, especially when plywood starts to disappear from the construction site of the cell phone tower (which passed a town vote by a narrow margin) and when a small fire burns the plywood at Everett's construction site (he has been hired to build a mini-mall on the former site that Value-Mart was interested in).

Tragedy befalls the residents of Riverlake on both a global and local scale. Hattie's dog Cato passes away of old age, leaving Hattie bereft and grieving for yet another family member. Readers are given a specific temporal marker when Hattie tells the Chhungs, who have not been watching the news, that the Twin Towers in New York City have fallen and that the United States is under attack by terrorists. While the Chhungs, survivors of genocide, react with equanimity to the unfolding events of 9/11, other Riverlake townspeople are not so sanguine. They connect the white van that stops at the Chhungs' house with possible terrorists (fueled by Ginny's suppositions at the local diner). Although readers will eventually learn that the van contains Sarun's former gang member friends who are trafficking in bear parts up in Toronto and selling them in Chinatown, the current mystery of Sarun's disappearance for days at a time adds to everyone's anxieties.

Events culminate one night when Ratanak, confronting his son over his potential illegal activities (which he believes are more of a drug than a bear smuggling nature), takes a shovel and hits Sarun on the back of his head. Sophy runs to get Hattie's help (this despite her previous accusations that Hattie is nothing but a sad and lonely widow who only wants to spy on them), and Hattie finds an unconscious and bloody Sarun, who is taken to the hospital for emergency surgery. Fearing that he will not last, the state allows the younger sisters to leave their foster care to visit their brother, but Sarun recovers and the sisters return to their respective foster homes. Shortly after her sisters leave, Sophy breaks down and confesses to Hattie that because she has believed Sarun to be an obstacle to her salvation and rebirth in Christ, she had, with Ginny's help and encouragement, started the fire at Everett's construction site, while Ginny fanned the rumors about terrorists and the white van that proliferated post-9/11. Sophy, under Ginny's influence, believes that she is doing God's will: "The Lord gave us this chance—I believe that. I mean, why else would He have sent the white van, right? Why else would He drive it right up to our trailer and put it right under our noses? Why else would He have terrorists attack America so people would believe anything?"[17] A contrite Sophy shares her transgressions with Hattie, trying to make amends for ignoring her as well as trying to right the wrongs she set in motion.

Chapter 4, "Everett: What Went Wrong," provides readers with the story of Everett and Ginny and what exactly went wrong—how things got to the point where Ginny has ended their thirty-seven-year marriage and is coaching a teenage girl to start a fire at her husband's construction site. As with Sophy's chapter, the heterodiegetic narrator uses the same speech patterns and verbal tics of Everett and seems distinctly different from either Hattie's or Sophy's narrator, particularly through the continual repeated phrasings that are peppered throughout the narration, as found in the opening paragraph about how Ginny has changed: "'Cause used to be, she was this sweet gal. Used to be, she was a gal no one would ever imagine getting mixed up with the Cambodian girl the way she did. And causing his trouble too, he's going to guess. The fire, everything, somehow. Causing it."[18] Going back to the time when Ginny was a sweet girl, the narrator tells us about Ginny and Everett's courtship, their marriage right out of high school, Everett's time as a soldier in Viet Nam, his combat wounds, and their early married life south of Riverlake in a city that had amenities such as a movie house and cafés and less snow. These are happy years for them—Ginny getting her teacher's license and Everett working for a construction company. Although they have difficulties getting pregnant and starting a family, nonetheless they remain hopeful and content.

Their troubles begin when they move back to Riverlake to help care for Ginny's ailing father, Rex, a man who got his nickname through his business savvy—the king of deals, as he is called—and who has an eighty-acre farm that, through his farming acumen and his real estate business on the side, he has never sold off. Unlike Everett's father, who was a poor Hungarian immigrant forced to be a jack-of-all-trades, a man for whom no work was too petty or humble, Rex and his family exude pride. Ginny and Everett take over the maintenance of both farm and Rex, but the demands are too much for them. When they try to work out a scheme to buy a mower and rent it out to the neighboring commune of hippies (two of whom, Belle and Paxton, are former classmates), they are betrayed by Rex's old friend Giles, the man who sold them the mower and encouraged them to charge the commune a rental fee that would take care of the loan repayments. While we are not told directly why Giles has betrayed his old friend, the narrator does relate a conversation in which Giles describes "how Rex had made a deal out of other people's misery for about as long as anyone could remember."[19] This hints at how Rex's successful real estate ventures over the years have come at the cost of his neighbors' misfortunes, as they have had to sell off acres of their farms in order to pay for expenses and taxes, which Rex has avoided through his own real estate business.

The bank forecloses on the farm when the family cannot make the payment on the mower, and Rex dies one night from a fall down the steep farm stairs. His last words to Everett are a command and admonishment, as he instructs him not to perform CPR on him: "You're a poor man's son who's made quite a mess here. But this much I think you can manage."[20] The cutting words at the start of this sentence will be repeated to Everett by Ginny after they have moved to a five-acre lot and after Everett has a custom home built for them. Ginny, who has found solace in the Heritage Bible Church, wants to open a coffee shop in their home called the Good News Café, a place where Christians can gather to be with other Christians. When Everett expresses reservations about this plan, telling Ginny that he does not want strangers coming in and out of their home, Ginny tells Everett that the money for the house came from the selling of Rex's farm and repeats the words of her father: "You're a poor man's son who's done good. . . . But this is my inheritance."[21] Like Rex, Ginny can see the world only through her own needs and wants; she cannot acknowledge Everett as an equal partner. In fact his refusal to be born again causes her consternation because she does not want to be "unequally yoked. She wanted to be married to a committed Christian. Someone who'd given up trying to do things by himself. Someone who'd realized what a lot of bad decisions he'd made. Someone who had put his trust in Jesus instead."[22]

Reeling from the death of her father and the loss of her family's eighty-acre farm, Ginny channels her grief and anger into believing that it is God's will that all of this has happened—that the commune and Giles represent the forces of evil and that all that has befallen her is a result of God's will rather than the choices she and Everett and Rex have made. Although the narrator says that Ginny and Everett should have split after her declaration that the house was hers, a series of misfortunes keep them together as first Ginny's brother and his wife die, leaving them to care for their young children, then Everett's parents pass, and then Ginny finds a lump in her breast. But after the children have grown up and after thirty-seven years of marriage, Ginny finally decides that she cannot be unequally yoked to a non-Christian man, which is why she kicks Everett out of their home and why she enlists Sophy in the arson at Everett's construction site. Everett believes that Ginny has a "blinding kind of vision" and that for Ginny, as well the members of her church, "they were going to set the world back right. . . . The world the way it used to be. . . . The world the way it was, back when [Ginny] was queen."[23] What the narrator alludes to here is that Ginny's embrace of the fundamentalist dogma is a psychological desire to return to a past in which she is still in charge, where she still reigns proud over her family's farm holdings because she cannot bear to live in the present and acknowledge her many losses.

Loss, how various characters cope with the myriad losses in their lives, is a running theme throughout the novel. We see the culmination of these losses, as well as the coping strategies used by different characters, in the final chapter, "Hattie III: The Pride of Riverlake." In the face of 9/11 and Sarun's hospitalization, the science-minded Hattie has not changed her belief that the reinterment of her parents' bones is part of her family's Chinese superstition, but she has decided that if it will bring her family comfort, then she would like to help alleviate their distress. Her niece arranges for a Chinese bone picker, Lenny, to meet her in Iowa, where he disinters the two urns of her parents and packages them for her in her luggage, which he suggests she check rather than carry on so that she does not run into problems at airport security. Having the twin urns of her parents in her house comforts Hattie, even as they remind her of her impending mortality and the mortality of everyone in her life.

Sarun is released from the hospital with a brace similar to the one his father wore on his back, and Ratanak, feeling guilt and shame over his actions, resolves to punish himself by sitting in a chair by the drainage pit, telling his family that he wants to die. Even after Hattie convinces Sarun to forgive his father, Ratanak continues to sit in the cold, venturing into the trailer only at night to sleep as the fall weather settles in. Greta and Grace, two of Hattie's walking group friends, try to help the Chhungs by dropping off food and then, at Hattie's insistence, posing as social workers, telling Ratanak that he has a complaint filed against him for being an unfit parent and that he will be interviewed by a state official in a month. The admonishment that Greta and Grace deliver to Ratanak in their social worker disguise rouses him into smiling and thanking them because finally he is receiving punishment from outside forces, and not just administering the self-punishment of cold exposure that his sitting by the pit was designed to do. Yet even after this censure by Ginny and Greta, Ratanak remains by the pit until Carter, who is also looking to help the Chhungs, comes by with an excavator to complete the drainage ditch that Sarun and Ratanak can no longer work on due to their injuries. This action causes Ratanak to rise from his chair and hand a cigarette to Carter in a sign of solidarity and gratitude, and the town rallies to support the Chhungs. As the narrator says, "Success! The whole town is giddy. Not that Chhung won't need support; already people are talking about an anger management course that addresses substance abuse too—kind of a twofer. It's in the city, but people are organizing rides for him via a sign-up at Millies. As for the holidays, Grace volunteers for Thanksgiving, Hattie for Christmas."[24] The community is helping the Chhungs to heal by embracing them as their own.

Carter's intervention with the Chhungs also reignites his desire for Hattie, as he comes to the realization that she is the reason he moved back to Riverlake. Though she is reluctant to acknowledge her feelings for Carter, they eventually find themselves entwined and united in helping Everett, who has built a hut on top of a platform on top of a wooden pole that directly faces his old bedroom window. Everett wants to remind Ginny that he is there—that she cannot shut him out. Hattie and Carter go to Everett to convince him not to press charges against Sophy, telling him that she wants to make amends, and Carter offers to reimburse him for the fire damage. Everett, however, sees the fault lying with Ginny and will accept payment and punishment only through her. He tells them, "I loved her but, well, now I just want her burned to a crisp see. . . . Now I'm aiming to send her right to hell."[25] When they return the next day to see if he has changed his mind, Hattie and Carter find that Everett has killed himself, asphyxiated by the carbon monoxide of his wood stove. Where Ratanak is able to accept help from the community and become part of the town as a way of coping with his losses, Everett's solution is to commit suicide as a way of haunting Ginny—his anger at her consuming him to the point where he sees his death as his only means of punishing her.

Everett's suicide plunges Carter and Hattie into a series of philosophical conversations that unfold in a single night, as they lament the various losses in their lives. After they drift to sleep, Carter continually wakes throughout the night to continue conversing with Hattie about what they could have done to help Everett, whether Hattie regrets leaving her life in academia to teach high school, and whether she shortchanged herself and her ambitions by not continuing her research. Carter tells her, "'You retreated, and worst of all, you never developed your capacities.' 'Developing one's capacities being, of course, the point of life.' 'It's as close to a definition of the good as we're likely to get, Hattie. You can say this is just another web of significance that I've spun, but it's a hard one to shake, don't you think. The notion that it's good to develop our capacities and bad to waste them.'"[26] This discussion between Carter and Hattie is the heart of Jen's novel—it is the "why" not only of *World and Town* but also of our lives—the existential question of what our lives are for. As the author said in an interview about the novel, "It's concerned with the question of how to live and what to live for."[27]

Toward the end of the novel there are two burials: Everett's and the interment of Hattie's parents' ashes in the Kong family cemetery. While the latter event is conveyed to Hattie by her niece, the former is related through the omniscient narrator as the townspeople, including Ginny, come to pay their respects to Everett. Ginny places a cross in his hands at the funeral home, only to have the ex-nun Grace discreetly remove it, after which one of the walking group friends observes, "It would've made him madder'n hell to wake up in heaven with that thing in his hand."[28] In the last scene in *World and Town,* Hattie wakes up in her home beside Carter and then watches Sarun and Sophy board the yellow school bus for the town high school. Hattie also thinks of her departed husband even as she recognizes her enormous love for Carter. Perhaps the greater message of the novel is that our losses are not replaced by the things we gain; rather they are layered together, so that grief and joy can exist in the same space.

CHAPTER 7

Tiger Writing and Other Essays
Gish Jen as Public Intellectual

Gish Jen's stature as a public intellectual is evidenced through her many essays, opinion pieces, interviews, and public lectures, some of which have been published in such esteemed national media venues as the *New York Times,* the *New Republic,* the *Boston Globe, NPR, Time Asia,* and *Slate.* Writing about topics as diverse as the bowdlerized version of *The Adventures of Huckleberry Finn* (Jen is not in favor of expurgating the infamous "n" word), the impact of Linsanity for Asian American youths, and a moving tribute to Steve Jobs that chronicles her evolution as a writer through her adoption of the Apple computer, Jen illustrates her active engagement with contemporary issues both literary and not, both Asian American and not. The wit, keen eye for detail, trenchant analysis, and lyricism that readers find in Jen's fiction are on ample display in her essays and in her latest book, *Tiger Writing: Art, Culture, and the Interdependent Self.* This nonfiction collection of essays began as a series of talks delivered by Jen at Harvard University, talks that were meant to provide her intellectual autobiography. However, the three interconnected essays offer much more than simply Jen's life as a writer; they also illuminate what she thinks about art and culture and the self. We learn not only what is important and interesting to her but also how she processes this information and why she is invested in the topics about which she writes. In *Tiger Writing* we are invited to see the inner workings of Jen's mind as well as the myriad influences that have shaped the prodigious scope of her literary output.

In a 2009 article for the *Guardian,* the feminist literary critic Elaine Showalter singled out Gish Jen as one of six prominent female U.S. American writers (among a larger list of about fifty, but as she noted, she could highlight only a few in the article). Noting that Jen "writes about great public themes without fanfare or pretension," Showalter also shared a quote from Jen in which she said, "I do struggle with the Asian-American thing. . . . I don't mind it being used as a description of me, but I do mind it being used as a definition of me."[1] Jen's nonfiction intellectual output serves to remind the general public that while Jen may be someone you would describe as Chinese American, she cannot be defined in such a narrow way as someone who writes about or thinks about only Asian American concerns. Perhaps more accurately, as a public intellectual who happens also to be Asian American, she demonstrates that her preoccupations fall into multiple categories; they may, for example, be focused on issues of ethnicity and race, concentrate on gender discrepancies in the publishing industry, or perhaps depict her admiration for recently deceased public figures.

Within the last category, readers of Jen's fiction may be surprised to see a tribute to Steve Jobs, which was published right after his death. In "My Muse Was an Apple Computer," Jen's writerly instincts allow her to identify with Jobs's impulse to continue working on a project until he got it just right: "Steve Jobs's perfectionism made perfect sense to people like me: Of course, he sweated every detail; of course he drove others mad. He was a J. D. Salinger who, weirdly, knew computing."[2] Charting the rise of the Apple personal computers that she used, from the Apple II to Lisa to Macintosh, Jen also discusses how her abilities as a fiction writer blossomed with the advent of personal computing:

> As for whether the Apple computers changed not only who wrote, but what they wrote, I can't speak for others. I can only say that these computers coaxed out of me an expansiveness the typewriter never did. For every writer, the leap from short story to novel is, well, a leap. It involves faith, and resources, and a conception, finally, of how much room is yours in the world. I was not a person who would have looked at a ream of paper and thought, "Sure, that is mine to fill up." But I turned out to be a person who could keep moving a cursor until I'd filled one ream, then another. It is a truly minuscule reason, in the scheme of things, for which to celebrate and mourn Steve Jobs. Still, I add my small reason to the infinity of others.[3]

This beautiful homage to the late Jobs is also a celebration of the legacy of personal computing that he left, and it is an insightful commentary on how his technological innovations have indelibly and positively impacted one creative writer and perhaps many others.

Tributes to J. D. Salinger, Alice Munro, and John Updike are perhaps more what we would expect a fellow contemporary writer of Jen's stature to contribute to the public discourse on American (or perhaps specifically North American in the case of Munro) letters. But what are remarkable in each essay are both Jen's intellectualism and her affection for the recently deceased writers and their works. She brilliantly dissects the popular and scholarly appeal of Salinger's *Catcher in the Rye,* noting that "one part of *Catcher*'s appeal lies in its purveyance of fantasy. This can, of course, have value—sensitizing an audience to the real limits of its freedom, for example—but can support solipsism, too."[4] Discussing the career of Alice Munro, Jen dispels any notions that the genre for which Munro was known is somehow too small or insignificant since "it is mystery that makes a Munro story: the mystery of her stories' uncanny rightness, and the mystery of her characters, a core wildness and unpredictability we startlingly recognize. And this, too, is where she transcends whatever particular appeal she might have. For however small the short story form, it is not . . . minor. In Munro's hands, it conveys nothing less than an ultimately unaccountable element in human nature and human experience."[5]

Writing about her mentor John Updike, Jen reminds us that authors, even those as well known and heralded as Gish Jen herself, are also readers who remain in thrall to literary giants such as Updike, who singled her out for distinction by naming her as his literary successor: "In 1999, when a British publication, *The Times Magazine,* decided to do a millennial special on 20th-century figures 'preeminent in their fields' and their chosen successors, Updike, for reasons I have never understood—please don't laugh—chose me." Fans of Gish Jen will of course not laugh because they see what Updike saw: a writer with an exceptional eye and ear for the comically absurd parts of contemporary life. Jen's essay in praise of Updike offers a metaphor that shows him to be part of a continuing strand of other great American writers, "a writer without whom the necklace of 20th-century American literature could not be judged complete," and she takes care to emphasize that his greatness was not simply literary but was in his very person: "I salute him, too, as a genuinely kind and generous human being. My editor, Ann Close, recently told me that for most of his career, Updike refused to take an advance from Knopf. He did everything in his power to help the house, and literary organizers of every stripe will attest to the time and effort he has poured into supporting literary culture."[6]

Jen too has greatly contributed to supporting literary culture. She was one of eleven prominent intellectuals asked to weigh in on a new edition of *Adventures of Huckleberry Finn* (edited by Alan Gribben) that expunges racial epithets by replacing them with more politically correct twenty-first-century versions. Jen's contribution, "Bringing Context to the Page," displays her trademark wit and humor, noting that the new edition could be seen as a collaboration between Gribben and the *Huckleberry Finn* author, since "Twain has, after all, collaborated with others before; did he not, for example, write 'The Gilded Age' with his neighbor, Charles Dudley Warner? This would just be the first time he has collaborated while dead."[7] In a meditative piece for the *New York Times,* "Inventing Life Steals Time; Living Life Begs It Back," Jen offers readers an inside glimpse into the tensions and challenges that contemporary writers face in trying to live their lives versus immersing themselves in the work of creating fictitious lives: "There is never enough time for writing; it is a parallel universe where the days, inconveniently, are also 24 hours long. Every moment spent in one's real life is a moment missed in one's writing life, and vice versa."[8] Jen attempts to quit the writer's life and describes her new world of gardening and lunches and leafleting, but what she discovers is that "I found life without work strangely lifeless. I wish I could claim that I went back to work because I had an exceptional contribution to make to the world, or because I found the words to dress down Old Man Death; but in fact I went back because life without prose was prosaic. It seemed as though the wind had stopped blowing. It seemed as though someone had disinvented music—such silence. I felt as though I had lost one of my senses."[9] For Jen, creating fiction is not merely work; it is an embedded part of her very self, as necessary to her as one of her senses, and her essay demonstrates the way in which writers who are committed to their craft must pursue their art because it is what allows their lives to be richer.

While it is clear that Jen writes about topics beyond what the public would pigeonhole as Asian American issues, she has also written about themes commensurate with her fictional oeuvre, such as ethnic identity, U.S. racial politics, and representations of Asian Americans in popular culture. In other words, though she may have said that she does not want to be seen only as an Asian American writer, neither does she shy away from this label. In one of her first nonfiction pieces for the *New York Times* magazine, "An Ethnic Trump" (which has been reprinted in *Essence* and the anthology *Half and Half, Writers on Growing Up Biracial and Bicultural*), Jen discusses the way that her mixed-race Chinese, Irish, Asian, and white son is seen as more Chinese than Irish—that his Chinese ethnicity trumps his Irish heritage. Jen provocatively observes in the essay's opening paragraph, "For as we all know, it is not only certain ethnicities that trump others but certain colors: black trumps white, for example, always and forever; a mulatto is not a kind of white person, but a kind of black person."[10] Here Jen is unafraid to talk directly about the assumptions our society makes about race and identity and to use outdated language, such as "mulatto," to reinforce her point about how language and race and identity have been inextricably linked throughout the last few centuries.

Similarly in "Who's to Judge?" Jen writes about the experience of finding herself as the only Asian American and nonwhite judge for the PEN/Hemingway Award, one made more fraught when she realized that Ha Jin would be selected as that year's recipient and that the past year's award winner was Chang-rae Lee: "As an Asian American, I was sure to come under at least private scrutiny for bias if these were the results. I was hardly dying to judge another contest, but would certainly not want to emerge from this one with a reputation for chauvinism."[11] When she expressed her concerns to her fellow judges and the PEN coordinator, she was met with skepticism and outright denial that race, hers or that of any of the finalists, should be a concern for her or anyone else. Jen notes, "They denied the complications of being a minority writer, partly to reassure me and partly, perhaps, to distance themselves from those who generate complication. I was not reassured, though, to hear suggestions that the social context around minority writers is not charged. It is. To deny that reality is to avail oneself of a privilege not shared by people like me."[12] Indeed, Jen recognizes that being a nonwhite, minority writer in contemporary U.S. letters is a lonely business, one that could potentially be mitigated by diversifying the field of writers: "I wished that, like my colleagues, I could leave this tour of duty as I had come in—as a writer, rather than as an Asian American. And I longed, suddenly, for the companionship of a fellow minority member. I knew that any minority writer would have instantly acknowledged the situation to be awkward and loaded. Many majority writers would have also; but how nice it would have been to have a minority writer, of whom I could be sure."[13] Unconstrained by political correctness or fear of professional repercussion, Jen boldly articulates what others may be too reticent to admit: that the life of a nonwhite writer in the United States is distinctly different from the lives of her or his white peers, reflected in the dismissal of the very valid and accurate analysis of the racial and cultural terrain she finds herself navigating as the lone Asian American judge.

Nowhere is the idea of the power of cultural representation and the necessity for having different types of role models more in evidence than when Jen writes about Jeremy Lin. Her essay in the *New York Times* about Lin's ascent and Jen's Chinese American brother's physical prowess offers an astute analysis not only of the phenomenon known as "Linsanity" but also of the complicated racial and gendered politics of Asian American male bodies, as the opening line of the essay affirms: "Most people watching Jeremy Lin these past two weeks saw Jeremy Lin, New York Knicks star; but I, watching him, saw someone else. That was my older brother, Bob, who, contrary to stereotype, is athleticism personified."[14] What follows is Jen's meditation on the differences between her

Chinese immigrant family and Jeremy Lin's Taiwanese immigrant home life, since Jen's parents did not encourage her brother's athletic pursuits (wanting him to concentrate on medical school and not lacrosse). She wonders what Bob's path might have looked like if their family had been more like the Lins: "What if my mother had sat on the sidelines with her stats, like Jeremy Lin's mother? What if my father had played videos of athletes for my brother to watch and imitate? It's hard not to wonder."[15] Lin opens up a world of choice and change; he defies the model minority stereotype of the Asian nerd forced into math and science. Through his example Jen sees multiple possibilities opening up not only for Asian American youths to embrace different futures but for U.S. society to open up to the reality of who Asian Americans actually are: "Who knows what will happen now that athletic Asian-American kids can say, 'Look at Jeremy Lin!'? And other people, beholding Jeremy Lin, might come to better appreciate how complex Asian culture truly is—how malleable, too, and how poised to enrich America in yet more surprising ways."[16]

As evidenced thus far, Jen's nonfiction illustrates her abiding interest in culture, art, writing, identity, society, and the relationships among all these elements. These various strains are pulled together in *Tiger Writing: Art, Culture, and the Interdependent Self.* Invited in 2012 to deliver the William E. Massey Sr. Lectures in the History of American Civilization, Jen presented three interrelated talks that provided a loose intellectual autobiography as well as a meditation on the cultural influences and tensions she faces as a contemporary American novelist born into a Chinese immigrant family.[17] *Tiger Writing* presents these lectures in three separate chapters (each roughly fifty pages long), along with an introduction, a few illuminating footnotes, and an author's note that explains Jen's design in crafting these lectures. Although the title, *Tiger Writing,* is not clearly explained from the lectures that Jen delivered, the work's subtitle, *Art, Culture, and the Interdependent Self,* becomes the predominant theme that Jen meditates on in all three chapters.[18] While these concerns are in some ways a departure, at least in terms of style and structure, from the narrative trajectory of Jen's fictional oeuvre, for anyone interested in understanding Gish Jen, *Tiger Writing* is required reading because the themes of her fictional works, the concerns Jen expresses for how characters learn to adapt to their communities amid competing self-interests, are the crux of *Tiger Writing.*

In the author's note, which was written after the lectures, Jen tells us that her motivation for accepting this invitation was "that despite thirty years of writing novels, stories, and articles, there was something in my bones I had not quite managed to articulate—a special way in which my cultural background was profoundly at odds with the literary culture I negotiated every day."[19] In the introduction Jen frames this tension as one "between an independent self that finds meaning in the truth within, and to whom rights and self-expression are important; and an interdependent self that finds meaning in affiliation, and duty, and self-sacrifice."[20] The three lectures elaborate on Jen's understanding of this tension, in terms both familial (the first chapter focuses on Jen's father's autobiography) and academic (the second chapter delves into cognitive psychology and the arts), with the last lecture (and third chapter) a culmination of the ideas and narrative strains of the first two synthesized through Jen's own fiction and her understanding of the art of the novel (in this third chapter she makes many references to her own writing as well as the works of other novelists). Taken as a whole, *Tiger Writing* represents Jen's intellectual autobiography (which was the suggested topic by the lecture chairman John Stauffer), but in keeping with the kind of innovative writer that she is, Jen does not present a linear narrative or a true autobiography that is focused only on herself; instead she uses the lectures to demonstrate her negotiation of independence and interdependence as the daughter of Chinese immigrant parents who now finds herself as one of the preeminent contemporary U.S. American novelists.

Within *Tiger Writing,* as well as in various interviews following its publication, Jen is extraordinarily careful to acknowledge the risk she is taking in linking (as she does) interdependence with a Chinese, Asian, or Eastern mindset and independence with an American, European, or Western personality. "I am aware of the danger of stereotyping," writes Jen in the introduction; "I am also aware, though, that fear of stereotyping has sometimes led to a discomfort with any assertion of cultural difference, no matter how thoroughly accepted by psychologists or how firmly grounded in research."[21] In the second chapter Jen spends a paragraph enumerating the many differences among Asian peoples, noting that their specific ethnicity, location, age, and income all play factors in their subjectivities, which would prevent us from claiming that all Asians behave the same, and she reiterates throughout her lectures that there are exceptions to the equations of independence = Western thought and interdependence = Asian minds.[22] Additionally, in both radio and print interviews, Jen has repeated that her argument is meant to be a nuanced examination of cultural differences rather than an absolute statement about the essential divide between Asians and non-Asians: "One of the reasons I tried to be so careful in this book is that when people are looking at something they don't understand they quickly label it as something that's from their own framework. And in the case of interdependence, the label is 'sheep' or 'robot.' You hear that all the time [about Asians]: 'They're sheep. They're robots. They're not human.' And I think that's where you have to be careful not to say, 'Well, it's true. . . .' That's the stereotype. You're looking at something, you see the phenomenon, but you make it into something that isn't really about the phenomenon at all. It's really all about you."[23]

Chapter 1, "My Father Writes His Story," illustrates the tension Jen sees between an independent self and an interdependent self by using her father's autobiography as an example of the latter. She opens the first chapter by declaring, "In 2005, when he was eighty-five, my father sat down to write his life story."[24] What Jen finds striking about her father's autobiography is not its brevity (thirty-two pages) or how quickly he wrote it (one month) but that the first eight pages, or one-quarter of his narrative, recount the genealogy of the Jen family beginning in 1131 with the Song dynasty up to the birth of Jen's father, Norman Chao-Pe Jen, on 26 June 1919. For Jen, her father's deferral even to mention himself or his birth until eight pages into his own autobiography is a prime example of interdependence; it signals her father's Chinese cultural mind-set because any autobiography must begin not with himself but with his family and the larger historic context of the Jen family compound in Yíxīng, which is in Shandong Province to the west of Shanghai.

It is truly interesting that in the first of three talks that Jen delivers, which are ostensibly supposed to offer an intellectual autobiography, she, like her father, chooses to begin by talking not about herself but about her family. Thus *Tiger Writing* models in its form the content of what Jen is trying to describe, which is the difference between being raised in a culture emphasizing interdependence, such as her father's, and being born into the culture of independence that the United States fosters. In the remaining chapter Jen reiterates the theme of interdependence and contextualization that her father's autobiography exemplifies. She notes the lengthy descriptions he makes about the family home: the geography of where it was located; the number and location of courtyards; and detailed descriptions of the interior of this four-hundred-room family compound. In Jen's assessment, her father's concentration on the family home as part of his autobiography reflects his keen awareness of the hierarchies that existed within the domain of his wealthy and powerful grandfather, a man who owned several businesses and properties and who, as the head of the Jen family, had utter control over the occupants in his home. For Jen, her father's emphasis on the physicality of his surroundings perfectly reflects his interdependent upbringing: "Before he describes any person, my father describes the power structure of his world as it was inscribed in its architecture."[25]

Embellishing on her father's autobiography, Jen shares with readers (as she did with her Harvard audience) more details about her father's family as well as her memories about the extended Jen family. She relates an anecdote about being "held back by a cousin, lest I board the minivan before the males in the family" as an example of the persistence of chauvinism in Chinese culture and the Jen family.[26] When her father finally gets around to talking about himself, his story seems to follow the more typical trajectory of the bildungsroman, as he describes himself as a poor student who was eventually aided by older brothers and a roommate, Mr. Chen, whose diligent study habits enabled Norman to pass the college entrance exams and eventually to graduate from the National Central University, despite the interruption of World War II.[27] Although studying in an atmosphere where Japanese bombers forced Chinese people into shelters (what Jen's father calls "disturbances") must have been troubling, to say the least, according to Jen's father, "the difficulties notwithstanding, 'the experience in the University [was] . . . the most valuable experience . . . in my life.'"[28] Shortly after recounting this declaration, Jen concludes her first chapter by telling her audience "that his overall narrative is nowhere near as linear as it would appear by my stopping here," thus returning to the theme of her lectures: that she, as the American-born and American-raised daughter disposed to a more independent framework, has crafted her father's interdependent life story into a more straightforward narrative than his actual autobiography suggests.[29]

Chapter 2, "Art, Culture, and Self," unlike the first chapter or the last, offers a more academic perspective about independence versus interdependence, as Jen tells her audience that her lecture will be divided into two parts, a science talk concentrating on cognitive psychology and an arts talk that exemplifies "how culture, small c, feeds into Culture, capital C, and vice versa."[30] Relying mainly on the research of the Cornell University psychology professor Qi Wang (and her various collaborators), Jen describes a series of experiments about episodic memory and self-narration that Wang conducted comparing Asian and Asian American college students with their Euro-American counterparts. Results showed that "contemporary European Americans, brought up to treasure their uniqueness as individuals, tend to tell long narratives about themselves that help illuminate, explain, and celebrate what is special about them, [while] Asians and Asian Americans typically do not."[31] For Jen, what is most interesting about Wang's studies are the ways it complements her notions of cultural differences between Asians and non-Asians as the difference between a reliance on interdependence versus one on independence: "Qi Wang's very striking, more general, and more literarily germane finding is that, brought up to define ourselves in relationship to others, many Asians and Asian Americans not only tend to recall fewer life events than European Americans but also tend to tell—and record—fewer, shorter, less elaborate self narratives."[32]

Using this as support for her argument that Asians (as personified through her father and as exemplified by his autobiography) come from a more interdependent culture, Jen next cites a 2007 study in which elderly Singaporean men were shown photos in which the background changed but the central figure in the foreground remained the same or another series in which the central object changed but the background was constant. The brain scans of the men looking at the photos in which the objects but not the background changed "show[ed] no indication whatsoever of brain activity," whereas their functional magnetic resonance imaging (fMRIs) showed changes in brain activity when they viewed the photos of the changing background but constant object.[33] Noting that this study is an extreme case, Jen nevertheless uses it as another instance of the ways in which Asians are steeped in an interdependent culture that focuses on the bigger holistic picture so that "figure and context form a unit from which the figure is inextricable," versus their Western counterparts, who "in contrast, tend to isolate the figure, perceiving it as wholly independent of, and eminently divorceable from its surroundings."[34]

At this juncture in her talk, Jen acknowledges that audience members (those present at the Massey lectures as well as the readers holding her book) may be having trouble accepting the culture differences she cites between East and West, Asian and European, China and the United States, writing, "But on to the objections many of you must have."[35] Indeed, for those of us conditioned to see the exceptions and ambiguities inherent in cultural categories and to eschew generalizations about ethnicity and race, much of chapter 2 at this point seems like a rehearsal of the general stereotypes that Jen, in her introduction, professed to want to avoid —that Asians were more focused on the family and their relationships to the community, effacing themselves for the greater good of the larger society. Anticipating the skepticism of her audience, Jen rhetorically asks, "Can you really talk about East and West like that, to begin with, as if they are stable entities, and doesn't the very word 'culture' conjure up islands[?]"[36] Citing the anthropologists Clifford Geertz and Richard Shweder and the psychologist Jerome Bruner along with factors such as class and social change as possible counterarguments to the studies she is quoting and the points she is making about independence and interdependence linked to Western versus Asian culture, Jen admits, "I have indeed, in the interests of time and dinner, presented a simplified picture."[37] Furthermore she emphasizes that the differences between Western and Asian people are ones of culture rather than genetics; she cites the people of Hokkaido in Japan as examples of Asians who show more independent traits and Mediterranean countries as examples of less individualistic regions to reinforce that her concerns are not essentialized into blood quantum but are instead about the cultural influences that inform a group's perspectives as either more or less contextual and community oriented, as either more or less individualistic and self-reliant.

In the second part of chapter 2, Jen shifts away from scientific studies to artistic objects, particularly looking at Western versus Eastern novels and visual art that seem to fit her conceptions of independence versus interdependence. Jen returns to one of Wang's research findings, that Asian and Asian American students exhibited less episodic memory, "the storage bank for personal events," than European American students, meaning that their recall of things in their daily lives was less specific than that of white students, who had strong episodic memories and thus could provide more detailed examples of their day-to-day activities than their Asian counterparts could.[38] Wondering if this translated into the realm of fiction, Jen e-mailed Dr. Wang, who confirmed that "European Americans include more episodic details in both forms of narratives [autobiographical events and fictional stories] than Asians and Asian Americans."[39] Jen then analyzes the opening of Marcel Proust's *In Search of Lost Time* as well as the preternaturally modern writings of Sei Shonagon's *The Pillow Book* for their elements of individualism, linking the form of the novel with Western independence. By contrast, and oddly enough as a reminder to her audience that art is not the sole purview of those of an independent bent, Jen turns to an eleventh-century Chinese painter, Fan Kuan, and his piece *Travelers among Mountains and Streams* as a model of interdependence (and she includes a reproduction in her book) since the seven-foot-tall painting features a craggy and powerful landscape of a mountain that dominates the frame, with a stream running at the bottom of the picture and with tiny figures of travelers and mules depicted minutely within the vast landscape that dwarfs them. For Jen, Proust's novel and Fan Kuan's painting represent the two cultures that gave rise to each artist, one independent and the other interdependent, with the novel, in particular, "very much part of a cycle wherein Culture reifies culture."[40] It is here, in the final pages of chapter 2, that Jen's intellectual autobiography, as we would recognize it in the United States, begins, as she tells us that she "was not a narrative native" and recalls her discovery of Jane Eyre, Miss Havisham, Sherlock Holmes, Lassie, and many other characters through her fifth-grade school library.[41] "Books were for me an Outsider's Guide to the Universe," declares Jen, and in chapter 3 she explains how her investment in novels helped to mediate the cultures of American independence and Chinese interdependence that shaped her selfhood.[42]

At the beginning of chapter 2, Jen tells her audience that she is going to emphasize "among other things, just how individualistic Western art and narrative are—a subject that will enable me to begin to relate how I, a daughter raised in a distinctly interdependent way, came to do a distinctly independent thing."[43] Explaining in an interview that she has perhaps overemphasized the distinction between East and West, independence and interdependence, Jen said, "I guess in this book [*Tiger Writing*], it comes up as more of a duality because I'm trying to introduce an idea with which many people are unfamiliar. The reality is much more gray. I'm trying to give people an idea of what black looks like and what white looks like before I introduce them to gray."[44] Chapter 3, "What Comes of All That," is the aptly titled final chapter, which offers a resolution to the tension between independence and interdependence that Jen established in the two earlier lectures. Here she presents the gray as represented by her own self: an Asian American novelist influenced by interdependent Chinese immigrant parents and by the individualistic novels of Western literature. Jen is the culmination of both independence and interdependence, as she said in the same interview cited above: "I'm a little bit concerned that talking so much about interdependence makes it sound like there's no 'I' at all in interdependence. I am clearly very hybrid, which is not the same thing as having two sides. It's about being a third thing, which is a hybrid. But there's a way in which I understand being interdependent, which I wouldn't if I didn't grow up the way I did. At the same time, I certainly understand what it is to be independent, too."[45]

Jen begins her third and last lecture by returning to her father's story—the subject of chapter 1. Picking up where she left him, attending university in war-torn China, she merges his story with hers, telling her audience how her father managed to leave China for the United States, was forced to stay there because of the Cultural Revolution, eventually met and married Jen's mother while earning his doctorate in engineering, and joined the faculty of the City College of New York. Readers familiar with Jen's fiction will recognize a loose resemblance between her father and Ralph Chang. Of course the characters and events in her fictional first novel do not map squarely onto her life, even though like Ralph, her father is an engineer teaching in New York City and, like the Changs, the Jens move from New York to Scarsdale (which Jen fictionalized as Scarshill). After sharing an anecdote about her father teaching a recalcitrant student a lesson in interdependence by making him take a garbage pail in and out of the classroom continuously until the wayward student repeated this action without questioning Professor Jen, his daughter flashes ahead to 1981 and her realization that there is another perspective other than her Chinese family's interdependent lens, which she discovers during graduate school: "And so off I ventured into the world of fiction, sanctuary of the independent self."[46]

Jen spends the remainder of chapter 3 demonstrating just how immersed in the world of fiction she became and how this world has helped her to understand her relationship with independence and interdependence. She cites a scene from her second novel, *Mona in the Promised Land,* that illustrates her frustration over the way Asian Americans are often assumed to be from somewhere else (somewhere in Asia) rather than from the United States. Mona responds to Mrs. Ingle's inquiry about where she is from (her initial answer, "The same town as you," being insufficient) by cheekily responding, "Deepest Darkest China."⁴⁷ This exchange emblematizes the hybridity that Jen spoke of in the interview cited above; here her fictional mouthpiece, Mona, provides the answer that Mrs. Ingle was seeking, thus reinforcing her understanding of the reciprocal relationship that exists between her and the Ingles since she is their dinner guest. Yet it also demonstrates the independence of Jen via Mona to lightly mock Mrs. Ingle and assert herself as an individual who cannot simply be boxed into ethnic categories (which is particularly true for this protagonist since she converts to Judaism).

Using other examples from her creative wheelhouse, Jen further shows how her preoccupation with independence and interdependence, with negotiating between American individualism and Chinese interdependence, has threaded its way in her fiction. She quotes from her short stories "Just Wait," "Who's Irish?," "House, House, Home," and "The Third Dumpster" and includes extensive passages from her most recent novel, *World and Town*. This last chapter is also a tour de force of literary allusions, as Jen references Henry James's *The Art of the Novel*, Milan Kundera's similarly and provocatively titled *The Art of the Novel*, Orhan Pamuk's Norton lectures at Harvard University, and quotes from H. G. Wells, Thomas Hardy, her mentor James Alan McPherson, William Faulkner, Virginia Woolf, the Chinese author Lin Yutang, the Chinese novelist Cao Xueqin, Sigmund Freud, Lionel Trilling, Saul Bellow, John Updike, Susan Sontag, and the poet Czeslaw Milosz, whose poem "Ars Poetica?" may have contributed to the title of Jen's Massey lectures. This catalog of influential novelists and intellectuals is a who's who of the Western canon and further cements Jen's own status as a public intellectual intimately engaged in her craft and deeply knowledgeable about the art of writing. Jen offers an insightful observation about the passion that drives all novelists: "So much of becoming a writer is called finding one's voice, and it is that; but it seems to me it is also finding something—some tenor, or territory, or mode, or concern—you can never abandon. . . . It is the thing that gives a writer, 'b.s. artist' that he or she is at some level, the chutzpah to drop the 'b.s.' It is the source of his or her 'authenticity'—this sense that however imaginative a work, the writer has a real stake in it, that he or she is driven by some inner necessity."⁴⁸ Although Jen never names the inner necessity that fuels the engine of her fiction, by the end of *Tiger Writing* it would seem that Jen's purpose as a writer can be gleaned by stepping back and looking at the bigger picture of her Massey lectures as well as her fiction. A driving force is and has always been her negotiation of her independent and interdependent selves, the crafting of the "third thing" that she spoke of, a hybrid self that is not bifurcated as Chinese and American but is instead the melding of the two.

Gish Jen writes about issues most pertinent to our contemporary lives, whether it is in an op-ed piece about tampering with an American classic, in a piece paying homage to fellow American renowned writers, or in a series of published talks that simultaneously reveal personal details of her life that are unique to her and yet resonate with all of us, demonstrating the relationship between self and other, between Asian and American as hybrid acts of creativity. Jen is a public intellectual, one whose Asian American identity and background add to our understanding of just who can rightfully claim the mantle of being a "typical American." As Jen notes, "I am writing very much with this idea that the American experience includes the Chinese-American experience."[49] In an interview about her latest book, Jen was asked about the "One True Thing" expressed in *Tiger Writing,* to which she replied, "We are made by culture, but we make culture too."[50] Gish Jen has clearly shown, in her nonfiction as well as her fiction, that she is a product of the Chinese immigrant culture of her family home and the American culture that surrounded her in school and her professional life as a writer. Her many narratives, whether fiction or nonfiction, also demonstrate that she is contributing to the culture in which we live: our contemporary American moment.

NOTES

Chapter 1—Understanding Gish Jen

1. "About Gish Jen," interview by D. Lee, 217.
2. "MELUS Interview: Gish Jen," by Matsukawa, 113.
3. Ibid., 116.
4. "About Gish Jen," interview by D. Lee, 217–18.
5. Ibid., 218.
6. "Gish Jen," interview by R. Lee, 218.
7. "Writing about the Things That Are Dangerous," interview by Satz.
8. "Gish Jen," interview by R. Lee, 218–19.
9. Smith, "Gish Jen: 'The Book That Hormones Wrote,'" 60.
10. While the author who transcribed this quote used a hyphen, the general consensus among scholars who study Asian American topics is not to use a hyphen. "Asian" is not modifying "American"; rather the term "Asian American" exists as a representation of a racial/political grouping.
11. "Writing about the Things That Are Dangerous," interview by Satz.
12. "Gish Jen," interview by R. Lee, 224.
13. Yardley, "Some of Her Best Friends."
14. "Gish Jen Talks with Scarlet Cheng," 20.
15. "MELUS Interview: Gish Jen," by Matsukawa, 115.
16. "Gish Jen," interview by R. Lee, 225.
17. Qtd. in ibid., 227.
18. "MELUS Interview: Gish Jen," by Matsukawa, 115.
19. "Gish Jen Talks with Scarlet Cheng," 20.
20. "About Gish Jen," interview by D. Lee, 220.
21. Ibid., 221–22.
22. Smith, "Gish Jen: 'The Book That Hormones Wrote,'" 59.
23. The other six novels featured include Theodore Dreiser's *Sister Carrie,* Edith Wharton's *The House of Mirth,* F. Scott Fitzgerald's *The Great Gatsby,* Ann Petry's *The Street,* John Steinbeck's *The Grapes of Wrath,* and Saul Bellow's *Seize the Day.*
24. Smith, "Gish Jen: 'The Book That Hormones Wrote,'" 60.
25. "Gish Jen," interview by R. Lee, 223.

Chapter 2—*Typical American*

1. Jen, *Typical American,* 3.
2. "Gish Jen," interview by R. Lee, 220.
3. "MELUS Interview: Gish Jen," by Matsukawa, 115.

4. Eder, "The Americanization of Chang."

5. Steinberg, Rev. of Jen, *Typical American,* 46.

6. Mojtabai, "The Complete Other Side of the World."

7. In Chinese culture, as in other East Asian societies, one's surname or family name is given before one's personal or individual name.

8. Jen, *Typical American,* 5.

9. Ibid., 4. Jen refers to World War II as the "Anti-Japanese War" to signal the way that China saw itself in conflict with Imperial Japan in the 1930s and 1940s.

10. Ibid., 16.

11. Ibid., 41.

12. Ibid., 47.

13. Ibid., 51.

14. Ibid., 57.

15. Ibid., 58.

16. Ibid., 61.

17. Ibid., 63.

18. Ibid., 76.

19. Ibid., 81.

20. Ibid., 67.

21. Ibid., 127–28.

22. Ibid., 92.

23. Ibid., 95.

24. Ibid., 104.

25. Ibid., 106.

26. Ibid., 114.

27. "Writing about the Things That Are Dangerous," interview by Satz.

28. Jen, *Typical American,* 158.

29. Huang, "The Redefinition of the 'Typical Chinese.'"

30. Jen, *Typical American,* 143.

31. Ibid., 147.

32. Ibid., 169.

33. Ibid., 179.

34. Ibid., 193.

35. Ibid., 194.

36. Ibid., 208.

37. Ibid., 202.

38. Ibid., 259.

39. Ibid., 260.

40. Ibid., 296.

41. Ibid.

42. Ibid.

43. "Gish Jen," interview by R. Lee, 226.

Chapter 3—*Mona in the Promised Land*

1. For more on the pigeonholing of Jen as a Chinese American and Asian American writer, see this book's introduction.

2. "About Gish Jen," interview by D. Lee, 221.

3. "Gish Jen," interview by R. Lee, 229.

4. Carey, "Switch."

5. Miner, "Asian-American Pancake," 36.

6. Eder, "A WASP-Free America," 2.

7. Yardley, "Some of Her Best Friends."

8. Ibid.

9. Ibid.

10. Furman, "Immigrant Dreams and Civic Promises," 214.

11. Partridge, "Reviewing the Literary Chinatown," 104.

12. Schlund-Vials, *Modeling Citizenship,* 122.

13. Jen, *Mona in the Promised Land,* front matter.

14. Ibid.

15. Ibid., 3.

16. Jen, *Typical American,* 3.

17. Jen, *Mona in the Promised Land,* 3.

18. Ibid.

19. Ibid.

20. Ibid., 10.

21. I have put "Orientals" in quotation marks because while this is the language that Jen uses in this section of the novel, it is not currently the term that is used to talk about people of Asian descent in the United States. As Jen says in *Mona,* "In another ten years, there'll be so many Orientals they'll turn into Asians" (6). Using the term "Oriental" to refer to Asian Americans is akin to calling African Americans "Negroes." Not coincidentally, Jen does refer to African Americans in this novel as "Negroes," but like her use of "Orientals," the term is meant to convey the vocabulary of the time period rather than the contemporary time of her readers.

22. Jen, *Mona in the Promised Land,* 14.

23. Ibid.

24. Ibid., 21. Unlike the use of italics in *Typical American,* Jen employs this textual difference to emphasize certain conversations as significant since all the italicized dialogue that occurs in the novel happens between characters who converse in English.

25. Ibid., 22.

26. Ibid., 28.

27. Ibid., 27.

28. Ibid., 28.

29. Ibid., 32.

30. Ibid., 190.

31. Ibid., 49.

32. Ibid., 82.

33. Ibid., 103.

34. Ibid., 109.

35. Ibid., 119.

36. Ibid., 159.

37. Similarly the independent Thoreau built his Walden Pond cabin on land owned by his friend Ralph Waldo Emerson, and he walked into town on a daily basis to be fed by his mother and to drop off his laundry with her.

38. Jen, *Mona in the Promised Land,* 159.

39. Ibid., 160.

40. Ibid., 169.

41. Ibid., 170.
42. Ibid.
43. Ibid., 171.
44. Ibid., 122.
45. Ibid., 123.
46. Ibid., 179.
47. Ibid., 181.
48. Ibid., 200.
49. Ibid., 203.
50. Ibid.
51. Ibid., 202.
52. Ibid., 203.
53. Ibid., 205.
54. Ibid.
55. Ibid., 206.
56. Ibid., 207.
57. Ibid., 215.
58. Ibid., 212.
59. Ibid., 220.
60. Ibid.
61. Ibid., 223.
62. Ibid., 225. In the beginning of act 4 of Chekov's play a character, Pischin, relates a conversation he has had on a train with a young man, who tells him that a "great philosopher" (who remains unnamed in the play) "advises us all to jump off roofs."
63. Jen, *Mona in the Promised Land,* 225.
64. Ibid., 227.
65. Ibid., 231.
66. Ibid., 242.
67. Ibid., 247.
68. Ibid., 246.
69. Ibid., 250.
70. Ibid., 251. When Mona tells her mother that she is not Callie, she refers to the way that Callie has suffered the indignities of not being her mother's favorite child with passivity and silence, whereas Mona, the big-mouthed rebel, will not tolerate such treatment.
71. Ibid., 255.
72. Ibid., 270.
73. Ibid.
74. Ibid., 272.
75. Ibid., 275.
76. Ibid., 276.
77. Ibid., 278.
78. Ibid., 292.
79. Ibid., 293.
80. Ibid., 293–94.
81. In Ho, *Consumption and Identity in Asian American Coming-of-Age Novels,* I provide an extended reading of the culinary metaphors within this scene in chap. 4, "Fusion Creations in Gus Lee's *China Boy* and Gish Jen's *Mona in the Promised Land.*"

82. Jen, *Mona in the Promised Land*, 294–95.

83. Ibid., 295.

84. Ibid., 301.

85. Ibid., 302.

86. Ibid., 301.

87. Ibid., 304.

Chapter 4—*Who's Irish?* and the Short Fiction of Gish Jen

1. Information about the number of places Gish Jen has had her short fiction republished is compliments of her curriculum vitae, which she generously sent to me.

2. I put "returning" in quotation marks because Duncan, like many Asian Americans born and raised in the United States, is living in China for the first time; he has never been to China and thus cannot technically "return" there.

3. Kakutani, "Free and Confused by Infinite Possibility."

4. The one exception is the unnamed narrator of "Chin," who is a teenage white boy who describes the lives of his Chinese American neighbors.

5. "Gish Jen," interview by R. Lee, 230.

6. Jen, *Who's Irish? Stories*, 114.

7. Ibid.

8. Ibid., 116.

9. Ibid.

10. Ibid.

11. Ibid., 118.

12. Ibid., 123.

13. Ibid., 125.

14. Ibid., 132.

15. Ibid., 38. In comparing the events in this story against the epilogue in *Mona in the Promised Land*, it would seem that this is a different Callie from the one described in Jen's second novel. The stories, I believe, are not meant necessarily to fit logically within the chronology and plotting of the novels but stand instead like alternate universes in the Chang narrative world.

16. Ibid., 39.

17. Ibid., 37.

18. Ibid., 46.

19. Ibid., 47.

20. Ibid., 48.

21. Ibid.

22. Ibid., 17.

23. Ibid., 20.

24. Ibid., 24.

25. Ibid., 25.

26. The slur "ching chong" has traditionally been aimed at Chinese in the United States, although other Asian Americans, particularly those of East or Southeast Asian descent, also find themselves the targets of this epithet. For more on the origins of "ching chong" as racist code, see Chow, "How 'Ching Chong' Became the Go-to Slur for Mocking East Asians," on NPR's blog *Code Switch,* http://www.npr.org/blogs/codeswitch/2014/07/14/330769890/how-ching -chong-became-the-go-to-slur-for-mocking-east-asians.

27. Jen, *Who's Irish? Stories*, 21.
28. Ibid., 30.
29. Ibid., 32.
30. Ibid., 30.
31. Ibid., 35.
32. Ibid., 36.
33. Ibid.
34. The Boston Museum of Fine Arts is a well-known institute and is commonly referred to simply as the Museum of Fine Arts. A Google search does yield results for other "Museums of Fine Art" in Houston, Texas; Richmond, Virginia; Tallahassee, Florida; and Montgomery, Alabama, but there are no markers to suggest that the family is from any of these locales.
35. Jen, *Who's Irish? Stories*, 101.
36. Ibid., 93.
37. Ibid., 97.
38. Ibid., 102.
39. Ibid.
40. Ibid., 103.
41. Ibid., 104.
42. Ibid., 106.
43. Ibid., 107.
44. Ibid., 108.
45. Ibid.
46. Ibid., 105.
47. Ibid., 107.
48. Ibid., 106.
49. Ibid., 107.
50. Ibid., 106.
51. Ibid., 110.
52. Ibid., 112.
53. Ibid., 113.
54. Ibid., 112–13.
55. Ibid., 113.
56. Ibid., 5.
57. Ibid.
58. Ibid., 4.
59. Ibid., 3.
60. Ibid., 4.
61. Ibid., 6.
62. Ibid., 11.
63. Ibid.
64. Ibid., 12.
65. Ibid.
66. Ibid., 14.
67. Ibid.
68. Ibid.
69. Ibid., 7.
70. Ibid., 15.

71. Ibid.

72. R. Lee, "Who's Chinese," 14.

73. For a trenchant and critical analysis of the immigration and naturalization laws that have circumscribed and contoured the lives of Asians in America, see Lowe, *Immigrant Acts.*

74. Jen, *Who's Irish? Stories,* 16.

75. Ibid.

76. Ibid., 49.

77. Ibid., 64.

78. Ibid., 73.

79. Ibid.

80. Ibid.

81. Ibid.

82. Of course the China described in this fictional story, which is clearly set in the late twentieth century versus the first decades of the twenty-first century, is no longer distinctly unmodern, as cities such as Shanghai and Beijing are more technologically advanced and cosmopolitan than many cities in the United States.

83. Jen, *Who's Irish? Stories,* 90.

84. Ibid., 91.

85. Ibid.

86. Ibid., 133.

87. Ibid., 134.

88. Ibid., 135.

89. Ibid., 138.

90. Ibid., 151.

91. Ibid., 191.

92. Ibid., 153.

93. Ibid., 162.

94. Ibid., 158.

95. Ibid., 187.

96. Ibid., 164.

97. Ibid., 171.

98. Ibid., 188.

99. Ibid., 189.

100. Ibid., 205.

101. Ibid., 206.

102. Ibid., 208.

Chapter 5—*The Love Wife*

1. The only member of the Wong family who does not get to narrate the novel is the biological son of Blondie and Carnegie, Bailey, who is thirteen months old when the novel opens.

2. Homans, "Origins, Searches, Identity," 73.

3. Kakutani, "Who's the Outsider?"

4. Seligman, "'The Love Wife': Marrying Mr. Wong."

5. Callahan, *Kin of Another Kind,* 148.

6. Chen and Yu, "The Parallax Gap in Gish Jen's *The Love Wife,*" 405. I tried to find the article that the authors cite, "A Conversation with the Author," but the link they

provided, http://jobs.imdiversity.com/Villages/Asian/arts_culture_media/qa_gish_jen_
1104.asp, presented with an error message.

7. Jen, *The Love Wife,* 13.

8. Ibid., 105.

9. Ibid., 42.

10. Ibid., 3.

11. Ibid.

12. Ibid., 193.

13. Ibid.

14. Ibid., 195.

15. Ibid., 155.

16. Ibid., 156.

17. Ibid.

18. Ibid., 7.

19. Ibid., 133.

20. Ibid., 60.

21. Ibid., 65.

22. Ibid., 106.

23. Ibid., 107.

24. Of course this does beg the question of why the Wongs choose China over Korea
or Viet Nam, two countries that would have been open to adoption at that time. While
one answer may be that they chose China given Blondie's fluency in Mandarin and
Carnegie's cultural heritage, the real answer is that Gish Jen made this choice for her
fictional characters.

25. Jen, *The Love Wife,* 129.

26. Ibid., 131.

27. Ibid., 71.

28. Ibid., 49.

29. Ibid., 147.

30. Ibid., 202.

31. Ibid., 213.

32. Ibid., 223.

33. Ibid., 240.

34. Ibid., 248.

35. Ibid., 257.

36. Ibid., 266.

37. Ibid., 280.

38. Ibid., 293.

39. Ibid., 316.

40. Kakutani, "Who's the Outsider?"

41. Jen, *The Love Wife,* 339.

42. Ibid., 341.

43. Ibid., 369.

44. Ibid., 376.

45. Ibid., 378.

46. Ibid., 379.

47. Ibid.

Chapter 6—*World and Town*

1. In *Tiger Writing,* Jen discloses that "*World and Town* pays deep homage to *Middlemarch*" (142), which is evident perhaps in the way Jen intertwines the domestic with the historic, as *Middlemarch* does.

2. Charles, "Gish Jen's 'World and Town.'"

3. Song, "Judicial Review #3: *World and Town.*"

4. Rifkind, "Neighborhood Watch."

5. Jen, *World and Town,* 12.

6. Ibid., epigraphs.

7. Ibid., 8. This prologue is rendered in italics, as are the retrospective memories that are part of Hattie's memories in the third chapter, "Hattie II: Rising to Fight Again."

8. Ibid., 11.

9. Leaf peepers are the tourists who come to see the fall colors; no see-ums are tiny black flies that plague residents in Vermont in the spring; and sugar season refers to the syrup that is harvested from maple trees. Of course one could argue that New Hampshire has all these elements, although given the emphasis on the northern topography of Riverlake, Vermont seems a likely candidate for Riverlake's geography.

10. Jen, *World and Town,* 32.

11. Graver, "Judicial Review #3: *World and Town.*"

12. Jen, *World and Town,* 94.

13. Ibid., 37. An interesting aside: Hattie's niece Tina is also the protagonist in an earlier 2006 short story, "Gratitude," published in *Ploughshares.*

14. Ibid., 111.

15. The reference to Crips and Bloods in this section suggests that the family is living in the metropolitan Los Angeles area, but it is never specified. Since the bus ride that they take to Riverlake seems to take only a day, it is unclear whether they are in the L.A. area, although this seems the most likely place given the concentration of Southeast Asian immigrants in this area.

16. Jen, *World and Town,* 191.

17. Ibid., 263.

18. Ibid., 273.

19. Ibid., 292.

20. Ibid., 297.

21. Ibid., 305.

22. Ibid., 303.

23. Ibid., 308.

24. Ibid., 353.

25. Ibid., 358.

26. Ibid., 368.

27. "A Conversation with Author Gish Jen with Bridgit Brown."

28. Jen, *World and Town,* 373.

Chapter 7—*Tiger Writing* and Other Essays

1. Showalter, "The Female Frontier."

2. Jen, "My Muse Was an Apple Computer."

3. Ibid.

4. Jen, "Why Do People Love 'Catcher in the Rye'?"

5. Jen, "Alice Munro, Cinderella Story."

6. Jen, "Updike Remembered."

7. Jen, "Bringing Context to the Page."

8. Jen, "Inventing Life Steals Time."

9. Ibid.

10. Jen, "An Ethnic Trump."

11. Jen, "Who's to Judge?," 18.

12. Ibid.

13. Ibid.

14. Jen, "Asian Men Can Jump."

15. Ibid.

16. Ibid.

17. As taken from the Harvard University Press Web site: "The William E. Massey, Sr., Lectures in the History of American Civilization at Harvard University have been endowed by an anonymous donor to honor Mr. Massey, the Virginia businessman and philanthropist. Mr. Massey was born in Ansted, West Virginia, in 1909 and attended the University of Richmond. At the age of twenty he began to work for the A. T. Massey Coal Company, and before his retirement in 1977 he served as chief executive officer of the company and chairman of the board. Mr. Massey was president of the Massey Foundation, a private philanthropic organization that supports cultural and educational institutions." Many notable public intellectuals have presented talks and published works of trenchant criticism through the Massey Sr. Lectures, including Eudora Welty, *One Writer's Beginnings* (1984); Lawrence Levine, *Highbrow/Lowbrow: The Emergence of Cultural Hierarchy in America* (1988); and Toni Morrison, *Playing in the Dark: Whiteness and the Literary Imagination* (1992) (see http://www.hup.harvard.edu/collection.php?cpk=1032).

18. Given the popularity of Amy Chua's controversial book *Battle Hymn of the Tiger Mother* (2011), it would seem that "Tiger" has come to stand in for "Chinese" or "Asian" in many pop culture formulations, including a piece by the journalist Wesley Yang, "Paper Tigers," written for *New York* magazine, which laments the rise of overachieving Asian Americans like himself. Yet one clue for the title of the book lies at the very end of Jen's final lecture when she cites Czeslaw Milosz's poem "Ars Poetica?": "So we blink our eyes, as if a tiger had sprung out / And stood in the light, lashing his tail"; she explains that these lines serve as a metaphor for interpreting novels: "We blink and see a tiger: and then there it is, sprung clean out and standing in the light" (Jen, *Tiger Writing*, 160). So perhaps the title echoes the trend of "Tiger" standing in for Chinese or Asian and is also a nod to Milosz and the interpretation of art.

19. Jen, *Tiger Writing*, ix.

20. Ibid., 3.

21. Ibid., 5. Of course this observation also begs the questions, which psychologists and whose research would validate these cultural differences?

22. Ibid., 57–58. She also cites the indigenous Japanese from the Hokkaido as one such exception to the equation of Asian and interdependence (74).

23. "The Big Idea #3: Interview with Suzanne Koven." For other interviews in which Jen explained that she does not want her work seen as replicating stereotypes, especially those that pigeonhole Asian Americans, see (or rather listen to) "When East Meets West

on the Page," by Marco Werman, on PRI's *The World,* and "Gish Jen on 'Tiger Writing,'" by Meghna Chakrabarti and Anthony Brooks, on NPR's *Radio Boston.*

24. Jen, *Tiger Writing,* 11.

25. Ibid., 26.

26. Ibid., 30. This incident occurred when Jen traveled to China for the reinterment of her grandmother's ashes in 2007, which may have served as part of the inspiration in *World and Town* for Hattie Kong's reinterment of her parents' ashes back in China.

27. National Central University was located in Nanjing at the time of Norman's matriculation; however, his university studies coincided with Japanese hostilities against China, in particular the bombing and eventual invasion of Nanjing (or Nanking in Jen's notation), which led university officials to move the university inland to Chongqing. However, as Jen notes, despite the move inland to avoid the bombing happening in the east, Japanese bombers made their way into central China, which Norman recounts in his autobiography.

28. Jen, *Tiger Writing,* 53.

29. Ibid.

30. Ibid., 58.

31. Ibid., 59.

32. Ibid., 64. I say "non-Asians" as Jen has on occasion, although she is more prone to rely on the label "Western" as a contrast to "Asian." However, this begs the question of whether either "non-Asian" or "Western" refers to African Americans, Latinos, or indigenous people, or whether, as in Wang's studies, the division is a racial one, between whites and Asians.

33. Ibid., 71.

34. Ibid.

35. Ibid., 72.

36. Ibid.

37. Ibid., 73.

38. Ibid., 65.

39. Ibid., 80.

40. Ibid., 98.

41. Ibid., 101.

42. Ibid.

43. Ibid., 58.

44. "The Big Idea #3: Interview with Suzanne Koven."

45. Ibid.

46. Jen, *Tiger Writing,* 112–13.

47. Ibid., 113.

48. Jen, *Tiger Writing,* 132.

49. "The Chinese Experience: Personal Journeys Interview with Bill Moyers."

50. "One True Thing: Interview with Jennifer Haupt."

BIBLIOGRAPHY

Primary Sources

Gish Jen. www.gishjen.com. Web site. 4 August 2014.

NOVELS

Typical American. New York: Houghton-Mifflin, 1991.
Mona in the Promised Land. New York: Knopf, 1996.
The Love Wife. New York: Knopf, 2004.
World and Town. New York: Knopf, 2010.

SELECT SHORT FICTION

"In the American Society." *Southern Review* 22 (1986): 606–19.
"The Water Faucet Vision." In *The Best American Short Stories 1988,* ed. Mark Helprin.
   New York: Mariner, 1988, 81–90.
"What Means Switch?" *Atlantic Monthly,* May 1990, 76–84.
"LuLu in Exile." *New York Times* magazine, 23 August 1998. Web. 11 June 2014.
"Birthmates." In *The Best American Short Stories of the Century,* ed. John Updike. New
   York: Mariner, 1999, 720–34.
Who's Irish? Stories. New York: Knopf, 1999.
"Amaryllis." *Paris Review* 179 (2006): 160–74.
"Gratitude." *Ploughshares* 32.2/3 (2006): 98–117.
"The Third Dumpster." In *The Best American Short Stories 2013,* ed. Elizabeth Strout.
   New York: Mariner, 2013. Kindle. 18 June 2014.

SELECT NONFICTION

"An Ethnic Trump." *New York Times* magazine, 7 July 1996. Web. 11 June 2014.
"Who's to Judge?" *New Republic,* 21 April 1997, 18–19.
"Inventing Life Steals Time; Living Life Begs It Back." *New York Times,* 4 December
   2000. Web. 4 August 2014.
"Sealed with a Click." *Yahoo! Internet Life,* February 2002, 66–67.
"Racial Profiling." *Time Asia,* 11 August 2003. Web. 5 August 2014.
"A Short History of the Chinese Restaurant." *Slate,* 27 April 2005. Web. 4 August 2014.
"Alice Munro, Cinderella Story." *The Daily Beast,* 12 October 2013. Web. 3 August 2014.
"Updike Remembered." *New Republic,* 30 January 2009. Web. 11 June 2014.
"Why Do People Love 'Catcher in the Rye'?" *New Republic,* 28 January 2010. Web. 1
   August 2014.

"Bringing Context to the Page." Op-ed. *New York Times,* 5 January 2011. Web. 1 August 2014.

"My Muse Was an Apple Computer." *New York Times,* 7 October 2011. Web. 20 July 2014.

"Spooked." *Daedalus* 141.1 (2012): 126–29.

"Asian Men Can Jump." Op-ed. *New York Times,* 16 February 2012. Web. 3 August 2014.

Tiger Writing: Art, Culture, and the Interdependent Self. Cambridge, Mass.: Harvard University Press, 2012.

INTERVIEWS WITH GISH JEN

"Gish Jen Talks with Scarlet Cheng." *Belles Lettres* 7.2 (1991): 20–21.

"*MELUS* Interview: Gish Jen." By Yuko Matsukawa." *MELUS* 18.4 (1993): 111–20.

"Writing about the Things That Are Dangerous: A Conversation with Jen." By Martha Satz. *Southwest Review* 78.1 (1993). Web. 11 June 2014.

"About Gish Gen." By Don Lee. *Ploughshares* 26.2/3 (2000): 217–22.

"Gish Gen." By Rachel Lee. In *Words Matter,* ed. King-kok Cheung. Honolulu: University of Hawaii Press, 2000, 215–32.

"The Chinese Experience: Personal Journeys Interview with Bill Moyers." *Becoming American.* New York, PBS, 2003. Web. 16 September 2013.

"A Conversation with Author Gish Jen with Bridgit Brown." Boston, WGBH, 2011. Web. 1 August 2014.

"Gish Jen on 'Tiger Writing': Interview." By Meghna Chakrabarti and Anthony Brooks. *Radio Boston.* NPR. 25 March 2013. Web. 4 August 2014.

"When East Meets West on the Page: Author Gish Jen Discusses 'Tiger Writing.'" By Marco Werman. *The World.* PRI. 25 March 2013. Web. 4 August 2014.

"The Big Idea #3: Interview with Suzanne Koven." *Rumpus,* 17 April 2013. Web. 4 August 2014.

"One True Thing: Interview with Jennifer Haupt." *Psychology Today,* 1 December 2013. Web. 6 August 2014.

Secondary Sources

"The American Novel: Novel Reflections on the American Dream." *American Masters.* PBS. Thirteen/WNET, New York. March 2007. Web. 10 September 2013.

Byers, Michelle. "Material Bodies and Performative Identities: Mona, Neil, and the Promised Land." *Philip Roth Studies* 2.2 (2006): 102–20.

Callahan, Cynthia. *Kin of Another Kind: Transracial Adoption in American Literature.* Ann Arbor: University of Michigan Press, 2010.

Carey, Jacqueline. "Switch." Review of Gish Jen, *Mona in the Promised Land. New York Times Book Review,* 9 June 1996. Web. 20 June 2014.

Charles, Ron. "Gish Jen's 'World and Town.'" *Washington Post,* 10 November 2010. Web. 14 July 2014.

Chekhov, Anton. *The Cherry Orchard: A Comedy in Four Acts.* New York: Grove Press, 1904/2009.

Chen, Fu-Jen. "Postmodern Hybridity and Performing Identity in Gish Jen and Rebecca Walker." *Critique* 50.4 (2009): 377–96.

Chen, Fu-Jen, and Su-Lin Yu. "The Parallax Gap in Gish Jen's *The Love Wife:* The Imaginary Relationship between First-World and Third-World Women." *Critique* 51 (2010): 394–415.

Chow, Kat. "How 'Ching Chong' Became the Go-to Slur for Mocking East Asians." *Code Switch* (blog), 14 July 2014. Web. 20 June 2014.

Eder, Richard. "The Americanization of Chang." *Los Angeles Times Book Review*, 17 March 1991. Web. 11 June 2014.

———. "A WASP-Free America." Review of Gish Jen, *Mona in the Promised Land*. *Los Angeles Times Book Review*, 26 May 1996. Web. 20 June 2014.

Friedman, Natalie. "Adultery and the Immigrant Narrative." *MELUS* 34.3 (2009): 71–91.

Furman, Andrew. "Immigrant Dreams and Civic Promises: (Con-)Testing Identity in Early Jewish American Literature and Gish Jen's *Mona in the Promised Land*." *MELUS* 25.1 (2000): 209–26.

Gilman, Sander. "'We're Not Jews': Imagining Jewish Bodies and Jewish History in Contemporary Multicultural Literature." *Modern Judaism* 23.2 (2003): 126–55.

Goldstein, David. "Page and Screen: Teaching Ethnic Literature with Film." *Pedagogy* 10.3 (2010): 562–67.

González, Begoña Simal. "The (Re)Birth of Mona Changowitz: Rituals and Ceremonies of Cultural Conversion and Self-Making in *Mona in the Promised Land*." *MELUS* 26.2 (2001): 225–42.

Graver, Elizabeth. "Judicial Review #3: *World and Town*." *Arts Fuse: Boston's Online Arts Magazine*, 23 November 2010. Web. 20 July 2014.

Harvard University. "Gender and the Business of Fiction: Radcliffe Institute." Online video clip. YouTube, 3 June 2014. Web. 4 August 2014.

Ho, Jennifer. *Consumption and Identity in Asian American Coming-of-Age Novels*. New York: Routledge, 2005.

Homans, Margaret. "Origins, Searches, and Identity: Narratives of Adoption in China." *Narrative* 14.1 (2006): 4–26.

Hopley, Claire. Review of Gish Jen, *World and Town*. *Washington Times*, 29 October 2010. Web. 22 July 2014.

Huang, Betsy. "The Redefinition of the 'Typical Chinese' in Gish Jen's *Typical American*." *Hitting Critical Mass* 4.2 (1997): 61–77.

Kakutani, Michiko. "Free and Confused by Infinite Possibility." Review of Gish Jen, *Who's Irish? Stories*. *New York Times Book Review*, 4 June 1999. Web. 2 July 2014.

———. "Who's the Outsider? Well, That Depends on Where You Stand." Review of Gish Jen, *The Love Wife*. *New York Times Book Review*, 7 September 2004. Web. 14 July 2014.

Lee, Rachel. "Who's Chinese?" Review of Gish Jen, *Who's Irish? Stories*. *Women's Review of Books* 19.5 (2002): 13–14.

Lin, Erika. "Mona on the Phone: The Performative Body and Racial Identity in *Mona in the Promised Land*." *MELUS* 28.2 (2003): 47–57.

Lowe, Lisa. *Immigrant Acts: On Asian American Cultural Politics*. Durham, N.C.: Duke University Press, 1996.

Miner, Valerie. "Asian-American Pancake." Review of Gish Jen, *Mona in the Promised Land*. *Nation*, 17 June 1996, 35–36.

Mojtabai, A. G. "The Complete Other Side of the World." Review of Gish Jen, *Typical American*. *New York Times Book Review*, 31 March 1991, 9–10.

Parikh, Crystal. *An Ethics of Betrayal: The Politics of Otherness in Emergent U.S. Literatures and Culture*. New York: Fordham University Press, 2009.

Partridge, Jeffrey. "Reviewing the Literary Chinatown: Hybridity in Gish Jen's *Mona in the Promised Land*." In *Complicating Constructions: Race, Ethnicity, Hybridity in American Texts,* ed. David Goldstein and Audrey Thacker. Seattle: University of Washington Press, 2007, 99–120.

Rifkind, Donna. "Neighborhood Watch." Review of Gish Jen, *World and Town. New York Times Book Review,* 5 November 2010. Web. 14 July 2014.

Rody, Caroline. *The Interethnic Imagination: Roots and Passages in Contemporary Asian American Fiction.* New York and Oxford: Oxford University Press, 2009.

Schlund-Vials, Cathy. *Modeling Citizenship: Jewish and Asian American Writing.* Philadelphia: Temple University Press, 2011.

Seligman, Craig. "The Love Wife: Marrying Mr. Wong." Review of Gish Jen, *The Love Wife. New York Times,* 3 October 2004. Web. 8 July 2014.

Showalter, Elaine. "The Female Frontier." *Guardian,* 8 May 2009. Web. 4 August 2014.

Smith, Wendy. "Gish Jen: 'The Book That Hormones Wrote.'" *Publishers Weekly,* 7 June 1999, 59–60.

Song, Min. "Judicial Review #3: *World and Town.*" *Arts Fuse: Boston's Online Arts Magazine,* 23 November 2010. Web. 20 July 2014.

Steinberg, Sybil. Review of Gish Jen, *Typical American. Publishers Weekly,* 18 January 1991, 46.

Tuttle, Kate. Review of Gish Jen, *Tiger Writing: Art, Culture, and the Interdependent Self. Boston Globe,* 28 March 2013. Web. 4 August 2014.

Watrous, Malena. Review of Gish Jen, *World and Town.* SF Gate, 24 October 2010. Web. 20 July 2014.

"The William E. Massey Sr. Lectures in the History of American Civilization." Harvard University Press. Website. 5 August 2014.

Yang, Wesley. "Paper Tigers." Review of Gish Jen, *Tiger Writing: Art, Culture, and the Interdependent Self. New York* magazine, 8 May 2011. Web. 5 August 2014.

Yardley, Jonathan. "Some of Her Best Friends." Review of Gish Jen, *Mona in the Promised Land. Washington Post Book World,* 12 May 1996. Web. 15 June 2014.

INDEX